*We invite you to a magnificent mediterranean cruise
exploring exceptional civilizations and sceneries.*

THE
MEDITERRANEAN

Terraced farming in the Balearic Islands.

TEXTS & PHOTOGRAPHS
ALAIN CHENEVIERE

THE MEDITERRANEAN

LANDS OF THE OLIVE TREE
CULTURE AND CIVILISATIONS

PUBLISHING MANAGER
ROGER SABATER

TRANSLATED BY
LENORE RIGUET

VILO

Although probably not a fisherman, this septuagenarian leaning on his cane and wearing the perennial sailor's cap epitomizes the strong love of life of the Mediterranean people.

Despite the tourist invasion, it is always possible to find pristine spots of wild natural beauty: here, ▷ a rocky promontory above the San Blas Bay, Malta.

INTRODUCTION
TO THE
CULTURE

EDITERRANEAN! THE WORD ALONE IS THE STORY OF THE SEA: 'THAT WHICH IS IN THE MIDDLE OF THE EARTH.' IT WAS KNOWN AS 'MEDITERRANEAN' TO THE ROMANS AND 'MESOGION' TO THE GREEKS; BOTH NAMES BEAR THE INDISSOLUBLE SIGN OF ITS ENCIRCLEMENT BY THE EURASIAN AND AFRICAN CONTINENTS. IT IS NOT TOTALLY LANDLOCKED, AS ARE THE BLACK AND CASPIAN SEAS, SINCE AT ITS WESTERN END, THE STRAIT OF GIBRALTAR, AN OPENING TO THE ATLANTIC OCEAN REMAINS, ALTHOUGH THIS PASSAGEWAY IS INEXORABLY BEING REDUCED BY THE PROGRESSION OF THE LITHOSPHERIC PLATES. THESE GEOLOGICAL CONSIDERATIONS, HOWEVER, ARE OF NO INTEREST EITHER TO VISITORS TO THE REGION WHO COUNT TIME IN TERMS OF DAYS OR THE INHABITANTS WHO COUNT IN TERMS OF YEARS. FOR THEM, THE MEDITERRANEAN IS SIMPLY THE MOST BEAUTIFUL SEA OF ALL. EVER SINCE PREHISTORIC TIMES, THE BLUE WATERS OF THE MEDITERRANEAN HAVE FASCINATED MEN, BOTH THOSE WHO LIVED ALONG ITS SHORES, AND THOSE WHO CAME TO VISIT FOR A SPELL. ANCIENT ROMANS CALLED IT MARE NOSTRUM, 'OUR SEA,' WHICH BEST CAPTURES THE COMPLEX FEELINGS OF LOVE, FEAR AND TORMENTED POSSESSION IT CREATES. THE MEDITERRANEAN MAY SEDUCE, SURPRISE, CHARM AND TROUBLE US, YET NO OTHER BODY OF WATER CAN COMPARE WITH IT, FOR IT IS OURS! THE POWER OF SEDUCTION IT HAS EXERCISED ON MILLIONS OF MEN AND WOMEN SEEMS QUITE IRRATIONAL. THE CHINESE AND THE AMERINDIANS HEARD OF IT AND DREAMT OF ITS MAGICAL SHORES. THE INHABITANTS OF NORTHERN EUROPE AND RUSSIA HAVE ALWAYS LOOKED TOWARDS THE WARM SUNNY LANDS

SURROUNDING IT. FOR THOUSANDS OF YEARS IT HAS BEEN THE OBJECTIVE AND SYMBOL OF THE EASY LIFE FOR MANY AFRICANS. TODAY THE WORD MEDITERRANEAN EMBRACES DREAMS OF TRAVEL AND VACATION FOR MOST PEOPLE THE WORLD OVER. ITS BLUE SKIES AND WHITE SANDY BEACHES ATTRACT INCREASING NUMBERS OF ADMIRERS. IT IS THE DESTINATION OF OVER ONE-THIRD OF THE WORLD'S TOURISTS, WHO BETWEEN JUNE AND SEPTEMBER VISIT THE RUINS OF THE MOST PRESTIGIOUS CIVILIZATIONS THE WORLD HAS KNOWN. THE MEDITERRANEAN IS A CROSSROADS OF CULTURES AND IDEAS. IT HAS BEEN THE MELTING POT, OFTEN EXPLOSIVE, WHERE SINCE TIME IMMEMORIAL PEOPLE OF DIFFERENT ORIGINS AND CUSTOMS HAVE MET AND FOUGHT AND WHERE THE THREE MAJOR RELIGIONS HAVE DEVELOPED AND CONFRONTED ONE ANOTHER. AFTER THE SUMMER, ONCE THE TOURISTS HAVE LEFT AND THE

The intense heat of summer does not seem to disturb the peaceful village life of Kilada in the Peloponnese.

NOISE OF CONFLICT HAS DIMMED, THE MEDITERRANEAN AGAIN BECOMES THAT UNIQUE REGION, GENEROUSLY ENDOWED BY BENEVOLENT NATURE, WHERE LIFE AMONG THE OLIVE GROVES IS GOOD. MEDITERRANEAN MAN LONG AGO MADE THE DECISION TO TAKE TIME TO ENJOY THE FRUITS OF THE EARTH, THE GENEROSITY OF THE SEA AND THE AMPLE SUNSHINE THAT BLESSES THE REGION THROUGHOUT THE YEAR. NOT A DAY PASSES WITHOUT HIS PRAYING TO GOD TO CONTINUE GRANTING HIM HIS FAVOR. THE DOMESTIC ARCHITECTURE, THE COOKING, THE COLORS OF THE FACADES, THE MYSTERIOUS REGARDS OF THE WOMEN AND THE RESPECTABLE WRINKLES OF THE OLD MEN ALL REFLECT A SPECIFIC MEDITERRANEAN LIFESTYLE. MEDITERRANEAN MAN JEALOUSLY GUARDS HIS ATAVISTIC PREROGATIVE OF LIVING IN COMMUNION WITH NATURE ITSELF.

TABLE OF CONTENTS

1

R. Campana.

THE REGAL OLIVE TREE

The olive tree is the symbol of the Mediterranean. There is about it an aura of legend dating back to ancient times, which accounts for the mystic respect in which it is held. This "magical" tree may live for centuries and still bear fruit; it is a source of nourishment for many of the people living along the Mediterranean shores.

The olive tree is present along the whole circumference of the Mediterranean where over the course of centuries many authentic "olive tree" civilizations have developed. The Ancient Greeks called it the "silver-leafed tree" and it has both given the Mediterranean countries a certain unity of appearance and has enabled different native peoples to share common values that transcend the usual national and religious differences.

Rape flowers enliven the sober silver green of the olive trees in Pamphylia, Turkey.

A half-open door gives a glimpse of an interior, in Rethimnon, Crete. ▷

THE LANDS
OF THE OLIVE TREE

*The wild form of the olive tree, the oleaster, has been known in the Mediterranean area since prehistoric times.
The tree as we know it today was first cultivated around 6,000 years ago in the Lebano-Syrian area of the
Middle East, the western part of what geographers call the Fertile Crescent. Some say it was cultivated at the
same time in Mesopotamia. Around 1500 BC it could be seen in Egypt and then in Libya which had
previously been buying its oil from Syria. Some time about the sixth century BC, the Greeks introduced the olive
tree to the northwestern part of the Mediterranean basin, while the Phoenicians introduced it to North Africa.
But it was thanks to the Romans four centuries later, that it spread throughout the Mediterranean area.*

THE HISTORY
OF THE OLIVE TREE

The *olea sativa* made its appearance in the Middle East early in the fourth millennium BC, when farmers in present-day Lebanon and Syria "tamed" the oleaster creating a hybrid that could be cultivated. Archeological discoveries have revealed that the olive tree was widely cultivated in Palestine, Cyprus and Crete as early as the middle of the fourth millennium BC. Olive oil was then considered a precious substance given to man by divine benevolence. Techniques for pressing olives were improved about 1700 BC in the eastern Mediterranean, with the use of stone rollers and a short time later, the invention of simple axle presses in the Syro-Palestinian area. Olive oil soon became the most important element of the various Oriental religions. It was also widely used in medicine and cooking. The Hittites bought it from the inhabitants of the Aegean coast of Asia Minor; the Mesopotamians and the Egyptians imported it from Syria around 1500 BC and it reached the Peloponnese 200 years later. During the course of the fourth and fifth centuries BC olive groves spread westward along both shores of the Mediterranean, reaching Italy, southern France, Spain, Libya and North Africa. At the beginning of the next century most of the Mediterranean countries were familiar with olive tree growing and all of them

used olive oil that they produced or purchased regularly from their neighbors. Mass olive oil production, however, corresponded to the period of Roman hegemony over the Mediterranean basin. Shortly before the Christian era its consumption reached a record high.
New olive groves were created in all the provinces of the developing empire, while enormous oileries were set up in North Africa. Each oilery could press between 5,000 and 15,000 kilograms of oil per quarter. All the countries of the Mediterranean world were now growing olives. The fall of Rome almost brought the oil trade to a standstill for lack of demand.caused a decline in the demand. During all the Middle Ages, olive tree cultivation and the oil industry of the western Mediterranean continued only on a small scale. There are no texts mentioning the tree before the 12th century. The Crusades were responsible for bringing it back into European favor. Italian ships controlling most of the maritime transportation between the West and the Holy Land began returning with holds full of jars of oil and young olive tree plants. Europeans became aware that there was a lucrative trade in that the liquid gold of the olive tree flowing westward from in the vast Middle Eastern stands. They decided to gain control of it while re-establishing their own production in the west. As a result the taste for olive oil survived long after the

end of the Crusades. During the 14th and 15th centuries, Pisan, Florentine, Genovese and especially Venetian merchants earned substantial profits from the oil trade.

It was the beginning of a veritable second "conquest" of the Mediterranean basin by the olive tree that continued for the next four hundred years. In the 16th and 17th centuries, while the number of olive groves multiplied around the Mediterranean basin, Spanish and Portuguese galleons carried the precious oil to the New World. At the end of the 19th century, despite the unstable political and military situation, large, partially mechanized plantations were developed in Turkey, continental Greece, Provence, Spain and Tunisia. For the second time in its history the entire Mediterranean area was cultivating the olive tree.

The fortified Andalusian city of Ronda is considered the birthplace of bull fighting. It is built on a rocky platform carved by the impressive Guadalevin Gorges that separate the two parts of the city.

The Bay of Idhra seen from the island's highest hill. This former pirate hideaway is now an artists' haunt. In the distance can be seen the Peloponnesian coast.

Current distribution of the olive tree in the Mediterranean area

The location of Mediterranean olive plantations has changed little since ancient times. The olive growing zone runs parallel to the coast, its width varying from 20 to 250 kilometers, except in Spain where its is cultivated farther inland in regions as distant as 500 kilometers from the coast. Portugal's olive production is substantial, but it will not be treated here, as it faces the Atlantic, and cannot be classified as Mediterranean. Bosnia whose shoreline is very short indeed, however, can. Greece's shoreline is immense, with the Mediterranean washing the continental coasts as welle as the Aegean and Ionan Islands for thousands of kilometers. Nineteen states border the Mediterranean Sea, whatever the length of their shoreline.

Following the coast in a clockwise direction starting in the west one comes to successively Spain, France, Monaco, Italy? Slovenia, Croatia, Bosnia, Yugoslavia, Albania, Greece, Turkey, Syria, Lebanon, Israel, Egypt, Libya, Tunisia, Algeria and Morocco. These countries have a total population of nearly 450 million individuals, of whom 200 million live in coastal areas. Some are "true" olive tree countries in that the tree can be found on over half, if not the entire, surface of its territory and olive oil constitutes one of the main resources.

The citadel of Victoria, one of the early capitals of the Maltese Islands,
accommodates the largest cathedral on the island of Gozo.

The citadel of Victoria, one of the early capitals of the Maltese Islands,
accommodates the largest cathedral on the island of Gozo.

This is true of Spain, Italy, Greece, Tunisia and to a lesser degree Algeria, Morocco and Turkey. In other countries olive growing represents a secondary but non-negligible activity: Libya, Albania, Syria and Lebanon are among these. Elsewhere, as in France, Croatia, Bosnia and Yugoslavia the olive plantations produce limited albeit high quality crops.

SONGS OF THE OLIVE TREE

All of the Mediterranean countries have, at one time or another in their history, extolled the virtues of the olive tree itself, as well as its fruit and oil. From the bards of ancient Greece to modern singers, via medieval troubadours, the peoples of the Mediterranean have always praised the olive in their sacred writings, poems and melodies. Here is Yahweh of the Bible advising Moses:

"Get thyself (scented herbs and ...) a setier of olive oil. Thou shalt prepare a consecrated oil, a sweet-scented admixture such as the perfumer prepares. Thou shalt anoint the meeting tent and the Ark of the Covenant, the table and all the utensils, the candelabra and all the accessories, the altar of the perfumes and the altar of the holocaust and all the utensils and the basin and its pedestal. Thou shalt consecrate them and they shall be sacred and whoever touches them shall be sanctified."

In the 5th century BC the Greek, Sophocles, honored the king of trees in these terms:

"There is a tree unknown to Asia and the great Dorian island of Pelops, an indomitable, immortal tree, feared by the enemies and thriving here, more beautiful than elsewhere. It is the silver-leafed olive tree, shining in Athena's bright regard, a tree that nourishes our children, a tree that no human, young or old, can destroy or damage."

In the 19th century the Italian, Gabriele d'Annunzio, addressed the beneficent trees with this vibrant prayer:

"Oh sacred olive trees, you who listen attentively to the roaring of the sea at ardent midday, oh you who listen to his mysterious words in the splendor of the sky, sacred olive trees, listen to Man's prayer. Oh you, *palladia munera*, you who are more holy than the grapevine, more sacred than the harvest, worthy

The imposing mass of Etna, the largest volcano of both the Mediterranean and of Europe, overlooks the superb Bay of Taormina. The origin of the city whose quarters dot the side of Monte Tauro, date back to the fourth century BC.

trees, grant us the peace you carry radiant within your bosom, your glorious peace, in your bountifulness, give it to my heart." At times the tone is more realistic, the concerns more down to earth, yet the invocation remains as heartfelt. The first century Latin writer, Columella, recommended adding olive oil to every dish to enhance its taste:

"It is enough to pour some on so that the dish does not dry. Moreover, it should be done every time a dish dries and loses its taste.

Seventeen centuries later, Diderot, the French philosopher and fine gourmet, wrote in the *Encyclopedia* the following, rather less poetic, lines concerning olives:

"When they are brought to the presses immediately after being picked one gets oil that is so sweet and with such a pleasant aroma that it is called "virgin" oil.... Besides Provence, Languedoc and the Genoa river where the best oils are gathered... quantities are produced in the kingdom of Naples, in certain islands of the Archipelago, in Candia and in certain places along the Barbary coast, on the Balearic Islands and in certain provinces of Spain."

Finally, one of the great poets of the twentieth century, Jean Cocteau, humorously praised the tree of good odors:

"Your breath one day in January
When, puffing heavily on your pipe, charming smoker,
Is it the train? Are they fairies?
The ashes of the dying day?
Let us be fair: it is the olive tree."

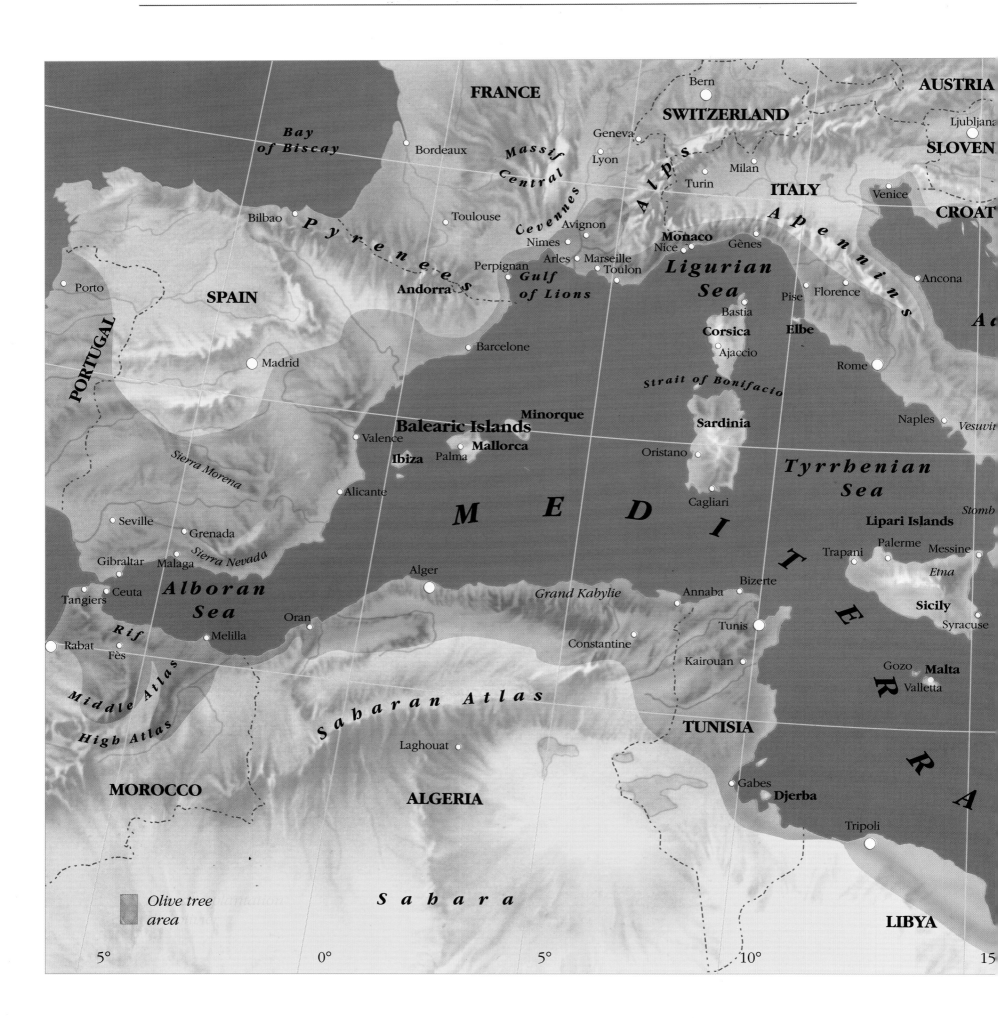

FRANCE

SWITZERLAND

AUSTRIA

Bern

Ljubljana

SLOVEN

Bay of Biscay

Bordeaux

Massif Central

Geneva

Lyon

Alps

Milan

Turin

ITALY

Venice

CROAT

Bilbao

Pyrenees

Toulouse

Cevennes

Avignon

Nimes

Monaco

Nice

Gènes

Apennins

Ancona

Ligurian Sea

Perpignan

Arles

Marseille

Pise

Florence

Ac

PORTUGAL

SPAIN

Andorra

Gulf of Lions

Toulon

Bastia

Corsica

Elbe

Porto

Ajaccio

Rome

Madrid

Barcelone

Strait of Bonifacio

Minorque

Naples

Vesuvit

Sierra Morena

Valence

Balearic Islands

Mallorca

Sardinia

Tyrrhenian Sea

Ibiza

Palma

Oristano

Stomb

M   E   D   I   T   E

Alicante

Cagliari

Lipari Islands

Seville

Grenada

Sierra Nevada

Palerme

Messine

Trapani

Etna

Gibraltar

Malaga

Alboran Sea

Alger

Grand Kabylie

Bizerte

R

Sicily

Tangiers

Ceuta

Annaba

Syracuse

Rif

Oran

Tunis

Rabat

Melilla

Constantine

Gozo

Malta

Fès

Kairouan

Valletta

Middle Atlas

Saharan Atlas

T

E

R

High Atlas

TUNISIA

Gabes

Djerba

R

MOROCCO

ALGERIA

Laghouat

A

Tripoli

S   a   h   a   r   a

LIBYA

Olive tree area

5°   0°   5°   10°   15

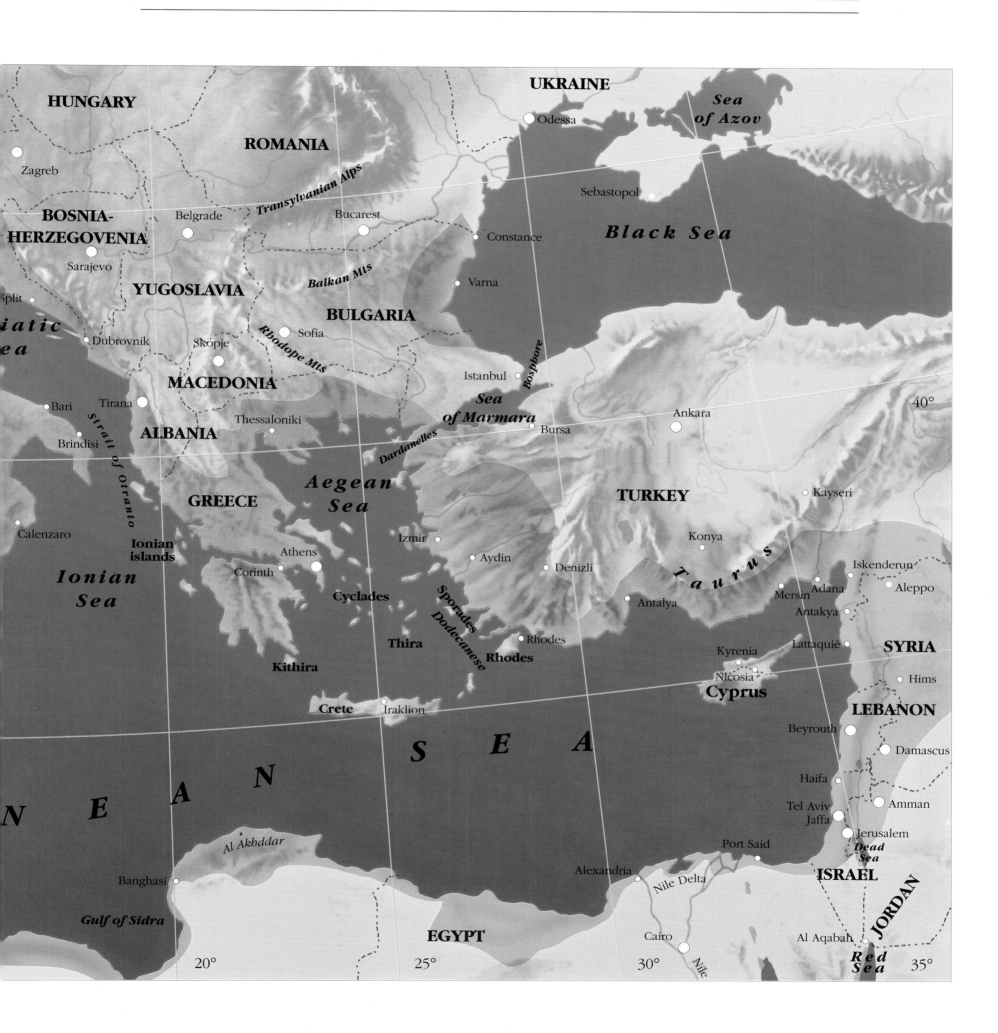

HUNGARY

ROMANIA

UKRAINE

Sea of Azov

Zagreb

BOSNIA-
HERZEGOVENIA

Belgrade

Transylvanian Alps

Bucarest

Sebastopol

Black Sea

Sarajevo

YUGOSLAVIA

Balkan Mts

Constance

Split

*iatic
ea*

Dubrovnik

Skópje

Rbodope Mts

Sofia

BULGARIA

Varna

MACEDONIA

Istanbul

Bospbore

Bari

Tirana

Thessaloniki

ALBANIA

Brindisi

Strait of Otranto

GREECE

*Aegean
Sea*

Dardanelles

*Sea
of Marmara*

Bursa

Ankara

40°

TURKEY

Kayseri

Calenzaro

**Ionian
islands**

Athens

Izmir

Konya

*Ionian
Sea*

Corinth

Cyclades

Aydin

Denizli

T a u r u s

Iskenderun

Mersin

Adana

Aleppo

Sporades

Antalya

Antakya

Thira

Dodecanese

Rhodes

Rhodes

Kyrenia

Lattaquié

SYRIA

Kithira

Nicosia

Cyprus

Hims

Crete

Iraklion

N   E   A   N   S   E   A

LEBANON

Beyrouth

Damascus

Haifa

Amman

N   E   A   N

Tel Aviv
Jaffa

Al Akbddar

Jerusalem

*Dead
Sea*

Port Said

ISRAEL

Banghasi

Alexandria

Nile Delta

JORDAN

Gulf of Sidra

EGYPT

Cairo

Al Aqabah

Nile

*Red
Sea*

20°

25°

30°

35°

Matinal Andalusian winter landscape before the sun's rays have warmed the frozen ground.

What other than the venerable "tree of the gods" could communicate
with the Greco-Roman vestiges in Agrigente, the illustrious ancient city of Sicily.

They say the olive tree never dies.
Its gnarled trunk sends down powerful roots seeking eternal life in the ground.

▷

THE TREE
OF THE GODS

"The gods have given us as a sign of victory, the dear olive trees that live near the androsse," proclaims a Homeric hymn. The ancient Greeks considered the olive tree to be sacred. Even three thousand years before our era, the early Mesopotamians and the Sumerians, and then nine centuries later the Egyptians, wrote of the virtues of the magical tree they believed to be immortal. The Bible represents it as the symbol of peace during the episode of the Flood. The earth had been transformed into a vast ocean. Once the skies calmed, Noah decided to send a dove in reconnaissance. On his second attempt, the bird returned carrying in his beak an olive branch, symbolizing God's forgiveness. This image has been handed down intact through the ages. On the verge of the third millenary the dove and the olive branch are still symbols of peace on Earth.

VENERATION BY THE ANCIENT GREEKS

The ancient Greeks were eloquent in praising the olive tree; they also contributed greatly to making it a veritable legend. Thanks to the lines of the most illustrious epic poets, it became a symbol of strength and peace. According to tradition, it was powerful Heracles who started cultivating the olive tree. After accomplishing the twelve tasks set for him by the angry gods, the now tired and peaceful hero is said to have gathered young branches of the oleaster and to have planted them in the hallowed soil of Mount Olympus. In *The Odyssey*, the great Homer depicted the olive tree as a symbol of fidelity. Odysseus left his home on the island of Ithaca 20 long years earlier in order to wage war against Troy. Penelope was patiently awaiting his return. One day, an old unknown beggar appeared before her. It was in fact her husband, disguised to fool the suitors who wished to usurp his throne. As he was kneeling at his wife's feet he reminded her how just before departing for the war he had built their bed from the trunk of a large olive tree that grew in their garden. Joyous, the faithful Penelope helped her husband to regain his position. Another even more revealing legend tells how Athens was founded. Cecrops' people had just finished the first building of Greece's future capital. Two gods, Poseidon and Athena, descended from Mount Olympus each hoping to give his name to the city to which a glorious destiny had been foretold. In front of the assembled population Poseidon struck a rock with his staff and a spring welled up. The goddess then proceeded to bring forth an olive tree. The assembly immediately chose the tree and called the city by Athena's name.

In historic times the Greeks' fervor for the olive tree never slackened. The sacred oil burnt night and day in temples and great quantities were offered to the gods and priests. During the Pythian, Isthmian, Nemean and Olympic games victorious athletes were honored with oleaster crowns and were awarded jars of olive oil. Just like the Phoenicians and Egyptians before them and the Romans thereafter, the Greeks never stopped boasting of the medicinal and culinary virtues of the oil from the magical tree. Sprains, influenza and injuries were all treated, pell-mell. Almost all of the recipes, particularly those handed down from ancient Rome, insist upon the importance of oil as the basic ingredient of refined cooking.

A SOLID CENTENARIAN

The olive tree is a member of the genus: *Olea* in the *Oleaceae* family. There are in fact over twenty species alone. The olive tree we know belongs to one of them, the *olea europea*, which itself sub-divides into two sub-species, the *olea sylvestris* or *oleaster*, commonly known as the wild olive tree and the *olea sativa* or cultivated olive tree.

The cultivated olive tree is an evergreen, whose size varies according to the climate and the soil. At the northern and southern limits of the olive regions, it is small and scraggy, but in the heart of these zones it is majestic with a thick knotted trunk sometimes exceeding 10 meters in height. It possesses a powerful complicated root system forming a large woody stock that acts as a veritable underground reservoir. This explains the trees exceptional resistance to drought and wind.

The olive tree grows slowly and blooms only after 8 or 9 years. Its life is divided into four different ages: "youth" from 1 to 8 years, "adolescence" from 9 to 40 years, "maturity" from 36 to 150 years and "old age" thereafter. It bears fruit only during the two intermediary periods, with production culminating during maturity. The vegetative cycle of the mature olive tree is divided into three seasons: awakening, maturation and harvest. After the winter rest from November to February, the sap rises in March and April. New terminal sprouts then appear and the blossoms flower. After complete florescence in May and June the olive pit hardens during the summer to attain its final size in October. As soon as the fruit is ripe, harvesting can begin. According to the speed of their maturation, which is dependant on climatic and geological conditions, the olives are picked from early October, for the varieties harvested when green, until mid-February, for the late varieties for oil.

The trunk of the olive tree remains smooth and gray-green during its entire "youth." Then, as the years pass, it becomes rougher, knottier and the color darkens to brown. This is also true for the branches which at the beginning have a square section and are light gray, even milky, before rounding off and attaining their silvery green color.

The leaves are persistent, with a life span of three years. From birth to death they keep the same lanceolar shape, ending in a macron, tinted dark green above and silvery-gray on the underside.

The flowers of the olive tree are borne in clusters in the axils of the previous year's leaves. The fruit, that is the olives, are called drupes. The endocarp or inner layer consists of a hard elongated pit containing an almond, whereas the epicarp or exocarp protects the fleshy oil-laden mesocarp or middle layer. The main characteristic of the olive tree is its remarkable longevity.

A traditional Mediterranean saying has it that "the grandson will see the olives produced by the tree his grandfather planted and his father tended." Indeed, the average life span of an olive tree is over 300 years, and often enough its disappearance

Cultivated terraces on the Isle of Mallorca, near the town of Valldemosa,
where Chopin and George Sand spent the winter of 1838-39.
The need to recover additional arable land from steep hillsides is a permanent feature of all Mediterranean lands.

Warfare did not disturb the peace of these olive trees in Istria, Croatia. The "patriarchal" size of the trees and the feeling of serenity they convey might well inspire humans with greater wisdom.

is due to the intervention of men who have either cut or displaced the tree. In fact, the olive tree is practically immortal to the extent that, once the trunk dies back, shoots develop at the roots, giving birth to a new tree. This is why, since time immemorial, men have considered it sacred and it remains shrouded in mystery.

OLIVE TREE GROWING

The conditions in which the olive tree thrives are related to climate and the type of soil it grows in. The tree prefers the Mediterranean climate, characterized by short mild winters, dry hot summers and fairly rainy springs and autumns, and especially the intense year-round luminosity of the sky.

Since cold is the foremost enemy of the olive tree, its area of existence is limited both by latitude (it is rarely found farther north than the 45th parallel) and altitude (it does not grow above 600 meters).

The tree will not support excessive humidity, which explains why it is found exclusively on dry rather poor terrain, such as limestone scree, colluvial lands or what is called the "red" soils on rolled stone terraces.

It is also susceptible to certain parasites such as the moth, the caterpillar, the jumping plant louse or the olive tree fly. The tree is robust and reproduces easily, an important characteristic for olive growers who regularly renew their stands when upper branches are damaged or in bad condition and when the trees no longer bear enough fruit.

An olive tree can be obtained from seed, budding, grafting and from root fragments. Despite its strength, the tree requires much regular care, particularly in winter after the harvest and again in spring, before the sap rises, when the tree must be given its biennial pruning. This spring-cleaning reduces the quantity of leaves and retains the best flowering twigs that will become the structural branches of the tree.

The inhabitants of Foggia in southern Italy have already spread their nets in anticipation of the coming harvest.

Although Greece is not the biggest producer of olives in the Mediterranean region, one sees limitless expanses of olive groves. Unlike other regions, agricultural areas are not cut off from villages but have, since ancient times, been an intimate part of the inhabitants' daily life.

Villagers in the Provencal region of the Drome harvest tanches, the famous olives of Nyons.

Olives are harvested at different times during the long ripening process

and this is what determines their color (green, violet or black).

The black olives in the jar will not be pressed for oil but sold for home consumption.

The Tihy mill, one of the oldest traditional mills in France, in the Paillon Valley. Its central axes and vats are three hundred years old. The owners patiently collected the parts of the original mill and rebuilt it near Lucéram, even reconstructing the wooden gears by hand.

OLIVES AND OLIVE OILS

Olives come from the pollinated white flowers and ripen from September to December depending on the variety. When the fruit turns from reddish to black, its internal transformation has been accomplished: the glucose is now oil, its clacium content is close to that of milk and it has a wealth of vitamins. Olives are grown either to produce oil or to be eaten as a fruit; in the latter case most are preserved The three types of olives - green, violet and black - all come from the same tree. The color changes with the maturity of the fruit and the time of the picking: green olives before ripening, violets at maturity, and black thereafter. To produce this full range of olives for the market, it is necessary for olive growers to harvest different

parts of their crops at different times of the year. The most highly reputed olives are the Sigeoise from Algeria and Morocco, the Dulzar, Manzanille, Mollar, Morona, Negrel and Sevillane from Spain, the Voliotiki, Kalamata, Throumba, Kathreiki, Amygdalia and Karyolia from Greece, the Amellan, Belgentieroise, Lucques and Picholine from France, the Ascolana, Cucco, Limona, Majatica, Nocellara, Sant' Agostino and Santa Caterina from Italy and the Barouni del Sahel from Tunisia. Spain is currently the leader among the Mediterranean olive producers with almost 655,000 tons yearly (one-quarter of world production), followed by Italy which produces 490,000 tons, Greece with 340,000, Tunisia

The olives are crushed in vats, virgin oil is extracted, the pulp is gathered and pressed once again to extract the remaining oil known as "first cold-pressed oil."

with 220,000, Turkey, 180,000, Morocco, 80,000, and Algeria 25,000. France brings up the rear with a meager 2,000 tons. Producers and oil millers distinguish between six grades of oil that differ in quality and price. The first one is virgin oil of which there are four sorts: extra virgin, fine virgin, common virgin and *lampante* virgin oil. All are obtained directly from the fruit itself which has been mechanical pressed using a procedure that respects thermal conditions so that the oil is in no way impaired. Next come the refined oils, which are derived from the virgin oils. The third group includes various simple olive oils, for which virgin and refined oils are mixed. The last three grades are all extracted from residual pulp; they are known as gross, refined and simple oil depending on the whether they were obtained by solvents, by refining or by blending respectively.

Annual consumption of olive oil varies greatly among the Mediterranean countries. For example, Greeks use 20 kilograms per inhabitant and Libyans 16, whereas Algerians consume only 1.2 kilos and the French 0.4. Despite medical research proving that the use of olive oil is beneficial to one's health, as the ancient Greeks already knew, its consumption remains modest in many Mediterranean countries where production is also on the decline. The reasons for this change are well known, and not surprisingly, are due to economic factors. Olive tree groves are not profitable. Oil is obtained only after long hours of work. It takes a minimum of 5 kilograms to produce 1 liter of oil and a good olive producer only harvests an average of 90 kilograms a day. Despite modern systems of pressing and a decline in industrial costs, the price of producing a liter of olive oil remains quite high. In addition, competition is stiff. Olive oil has been replaced in North Africa by American soy oil and in the Middle East by Malaysian palm oil. Despite protective measures adopted by the European Union in favor of olive oil, local rivals such as sunflower oil, peanut oil, rape oil and cotton oil are are proving a serious threat. Olive oil now only represents 4% of world trade in oilseeds and it has progressed over the last five years at an average rate of only 1.3% per annum whereas other vegetable oils have attained 4.5%.

It is quite likely that olive oil will become a luxury product for the privileged few, in which case people of the southern shores of the Mediterranean may no longer be able to afford it.

The Ramade family oil mill in Nyons is a traditional, but more industrialized, mill. It was built in 1904 when southeastern France's oil production was at its height.

2

A COMPLEX SEA

TWO HUNDRED AND TWENTY-FIVE MILLION YEARS AGO ALL THE CONTINENTS WERE JOINED IN A SINGLE MASS THAT GEOGRAPHERS CALLED "PANGAEA" OR "TOTAL EARTH", WHICH WAS SURROUNDED BY A SINGLE SEA, "PANTHALASSA" OR "TOTAL SEA." THE TWO GREAT TECTONIC PLATES THAT SUPPORTED THIS ENORMOUS MASS THEN BEGAN TO SEPARATE, ALLOWING GONDWANA TO SLIDE TO THE SOUTH AND LAURASIA TO THE NORTH. GEOGRAPHERS NAMED THE IMMENSE SEA THAT GIRDLED THE EARTH AND SEPARATED THESE TWO SUPERCONTINENTS TETHYS FOR THE GREEK GODDESS OF THE SAME NAME, DAUGHTER OF THE SKY AND THE EARTH, WHO SYMBOLIZED THE NURTURING SEA. OVER THE COURSE OF MILLIONS OF YEARS, THE LITHOSPHERIC PLATES CONTINUED TO DRIFT CAUSING GONDWANA AND LAURASIA TO BREAK INTO PIECES; THE ATLANTIC OCEAN OPENED AND TETHYS SHRANK, LEAVING THE MEDITERRANEAN AS ITS LAST REMNANT.

Sunset over the jagged ridges of the Troodos Mountains, in Cyprus.

*The Island of Vulcano, traditionally believed to be the home of the God Aeolus,
slowly emerges from the morning mist in autumn.* ▷

A FIERY VIOLENT BIRTH

The genesis of the Mediterranean Sea is unequaled in the history of the earth. It is unique in the violence of the events that mark its life story. No other ocean or sea underwent such upheavals and reversals during its creation. Under the seductive blue waters of the Romans' Mare Nostrum are deeply engraved scars bearing testimony to the sea's dramatic birth. The sea died and was partially "miraculously" reborn over and over again. Never calm, never spared geological upheavals, constantly raised, broken, and split apart, the Mediterranean basin has never had a peaceful existence. Nor is it likely to soon!

ITS FIRST BRIEF TORMENTED LIFE

It all began some 30 million years ago, as Eurasia, part of the former Laurasia, was caught up in colossal tellurian collisions, which slowly gave it its original appearance. Although greatly reduced in comparison to its original size, Tethys, still opened at its western end onto the Atlantic and at its east onto the Indian Ocean. The African plate collided with the central part of the Eurasian plate, slightly to the east of the present-day Middle East, causing deep geological upheavals. Mountains rose up, enormous rift valleys appeared, while the eastern water passage closed definitively. Blocked by the lands of Arabia to the east, the African plate, responding to the enormous pressure of the land mantle, then "skidded" in a vast circular movement which brought its western extremity up towards today's Iberian peninsula. Shortly thereafter the African and Eurasian plates joined, creating the Strait of Gibraltar and closing the western entrance to the waters of the Atlantic.

The first Mediterranean Sea was born literally trapped between the two lithospheric plates. As the movement of the African plate continued, a third collision was soon to bring about the emergence of Sicily, Calabria and the mountains of Apulia, thus further reducing the size of the Mediterranean basin. Even at the time of its violent birth the first Mediterranean's death sentenced was signed, for it was completely landlocked. The African plate was well lodged under its Eurasian counterpart in both the east and the west, and was continuing its thrust northward, and thus submitting the Tethys-Mediterranean sea floor to phenomena of considerable pressure and uprisings. Around seven million years ago the surface of the sea was subjected to intense evaporation causing a constant lowering of the water level. The climate was also quite different from the one we know today. Temperatures were superior by 12 to 13 degrees Celsius and the evaporation rate was significantly higher as well. This early Mediterranean was bound to disappear rapidly. Specialists believe that it vanished in fewer than 500 years.

They were able to put forward such a surprising figure by studying what is taking place at the present time. Indeed, contemporary measurements show that each year the sea loses nearly 4,000 square kilometers of water, despite inflows from the Atlantic and the great Mediterranean rivers, the Ebre, the Rhône, the Po and the Nile, to mention only the most famous. This implies that, if the threshold of Gibraltar were to close again, and if present conditions prevailed, albeit with colder temperatures, the Mediterranean might well go dry in 1,000 years.

This is the story of how the first Mediterranean dried up, leaving vertiginous cliffs around its perimeter and in its center, lakes whose salinity was so exceptionally high that all forms of life ceased. The salt content of the current Mediterranean already reaches an average of 38 parts per thousand, increasing progressively from west to east - 36.5 parts per thousand in the Alboran Sea and 39.5 parts per thousand in the Levantine basin.

One can thus imagine the extent of the ecological catastrophe of the Tertiary Era.

OTHER EXISTENCES

Until recently the scientific community preferred the explanation of a new geological upheaval that took place around six million years ago, when the Gibraltar lock suddenly ceded and the waters of the Atlantic rushed, in a 3,000-meter-high cascade, into the Mediterranean desert below. Today this hypothesis has almost unanimously been abandoned. We now know that the sea floor was only 1,000 to 1,5000 meters below the surface of the water, and that when the primitive Mediterranean disappeared, its basin was never totally dry, but continued to shelter residual over-salty lakes. New discoveries have profoundly altered our previous suppositions about the Mediterranean's genesis, notably the 1970 Glomar-Challenger mission that revealed a number of revolutionary findings. Scientists noted that the sea substratum contains, in deep layers hidden under recent marine sediments, greater quantities of evaporite salts than those currently dissolved in the water. In certain places these saline deposits reach 1,5 kilometers in depth. Drilling revealed that they all contain microscopic algae fossils. Since algae are organisms that cannot survive in deep water, because their main vital functions are dependent on the sun's rays, it is obvious that these saline deposits must have been created in shallow water. This means that the original Mediterranean did not dry up only once, but rather in several stages! Different explanations have been put forward to account for these successive, more or less partial, deaths and the alternating, unequal periods of rebirths. The principal one is related to the proximity of the Atlantic Ocean which succeeded several times in "stepping over" the shallow barrier - 15 kilometers wide and on the average 320 meters deep - the threshold of Gibraltar. The most recent flood took place a little less than 6 million years ago. This colossal tellurian movement pushing northwards along the African plate cut through the rocky thrusts held in place by the mass of the relatively stable Eurasian plate causing the "bridge" between Spain and Morocco to break into several pieces and revealing deep faults. The waters of the Atlantic surged massively into these faults, giving birth to today's Mediterranean.

MARE NOSTRUM

"Our Sea" today covers a surface of slightly over 2.5 million square kilometers, which represents only 0.8% of the world's hydrosphere. Its average depth is less than 1,5000 meters. The rare, extremely reduced, continental shelves are located along the Spanish coast, in the Gulfs of Lion and Gabes, in the northern and middle Adriatic, off the Nile delta and in the Aegean Sea. There are, on the other hand, several zones of deep troughs arranged in a series of crescents, varying from a depth of 4,000 meters in the southwest to 5,121 meters in the Peloponnese. Oceanographers divide the Mediterranean into the western and the eastern basins, separated by the Sicilian-Tunisian straits that scarcely exceed 400 meters in depth. The volume of water in the Mediterranean is estimated at 3,700,000 square kilometers, and is fed and renewed by four different sources: the Atlantic, the great rivers, the Sea of Marmara and the Black Sea, and finally by rainwater. Thanks to the Gibraltar threshold, the Mediterranean's principal "lifeline", there is an exchange of over 1,5000,000 square meters of water per second. The net inflow from the Atlantic amounts to 41,000 square meters per second, whereas that of the great rivers accounts for 15,000 square meters. The Sea of Marmara and the Black Sea bring only 6,000 square meters, which is really very little compared to the 31,000 square meters of rainwater during the same period. This total inflow is equaled, if not exceeded by, evaporation that each year causes the elimination of 2,9000 square kilometers of water! During the last two decades relatively small deficits have been recorded in the Mediterranean. For the last four years, however, a slight increase has been recorded, which tends to confirm the instability of the Mediterranean milieu.

The two most tormented geological zones on the Mediterranean are in the Franco-Algerian Basin and the Greco-Libyan Basin, where there are numerous volcanoes: Vesuvius, Etna, Stromboli and Santorin. Earthquakes are frequent in northern Italy, Croatia, Algeria and Morocco. Remarkable studies conducted by French oceanographers have linked the extraordinary seismic activity in these two regions to the "void" still remaining under the African and Eurasian plates. This void exists where the two plates have not yet directly met. It is, however, rapidly disappearing. The crash is already programmed. If nothing stops the African plate, its entire facade will collide with Eurasia in 15 million years. The collision may even occur sooner if, as in the past,

the level of the Mediterranean drops as a result of the general warming of the earth and if rainfall and the great rivers of the Mediterranean perimeter are no longer able to offset the intense evaporation. In fact, the phenomenon is even believed to be accelerating, since the lower water level results in the rise of the Trafalgar barrier, thus eventually completely obstructing the western opening.

Indisputably, our beautiful blue sea is in the throes of death. Inexorably, it will vanish from world maps, taking with it the last traces of ancient Tethys.

The central crater of Vesuvius. This southern Italian volcano, culminating at 1277 meters, is still active. It erupted in 79AD killing thousands and burying several Roman cities including Pompeii.

The high-rising summits of the Djurdjura along the Mediterranean side of Great Kabylie, Algeria.

THE FUTURE MEDITERRANEAN

The high Gibraltar threshold keeps cold Atlantic deepwater, with its wealth of fish and plankton from entering the Mediterranean. For at least five million years the contributions from the Atlantic have varied according to the planet's climatic changes. During the long glaciations of the Quaternary Era, when the Mediterranean lacked water, a strong surface current evacuated the water towards the west, whereas deep currents ran in the opposite direction, allowing boreal species to enter the Mediterranean. Conversely, during the warming periods such as the present time, incoming easterly surface currents are strong, while weaker deeper counter-currents move westward. Finally, like every closed sea, and the Mediterranean is on the verge of becoming one, the rate of salinity is higher than the oceans (37 to 38 grams of salt per liter as compared to 34.7) and there is a lack of mineral salts due to weak deepwater circulation.

The presence of nitrogen and phosphorus compounds, the veritable "fertilizers" of vegetable life, is the feeblest of all the earth's seas. As a consequence there is a great paucity of microscopic plankton algae in the Mediterranean marine milieu, which in turn raises serious problems concerning the number of individuals per species. Is the Mediterranean likely to experience a calmer existence than in the past? The answer is no, because there has been no slowing down of the original phenomena. The African plate is continuing to drift northward at the rate of one centimeter per year. The sea is continuing, therefore, to shrink as the plate advances. After bracing itself against the Eurasian plate, it is now sliding under it, in the west under the Iberian Peninsula and in the east under Arabia. This subduction is the cause of the earthquakes and volcanic eruptions that regularly affect the perimeter of the Mediterranean, as well as of the incessant submarine upheavals.

The long pristine beaches of the Bay of Bueb in Libya, are irresistible invitations to bathe.

*The hundred or so remaining Lebanese cedars that once brought wealth and renown to the land
are now protected in a national reserve.*

The wild backcountry of the Corsican mountains near Corte.

The bay of Vivari in Greece is one of the least frequented paradises of the eastern Peloponnesus.

A rosemary plant (the Latin "rosmariunus" means "sea dew") is found in such great abundance around the Mediterranean ▷
that it has become one of its symbols.

MIXED FLORA AND FAUNA

This traumatic geological life engendered distinctive flora and fauna. No living marine species were able to survive the phenomena of parching and oversalinization that accompanied the great upheavals at the end of the Tertiary Era. Landmasses increased with each successive drop in the water level, creating new bridges between continents. Animal and vegetal species came into contact that otherwise would have remained apart. Some disappeared, others managed to cohabit, while still others mixed and produced new forms of life. Consequently, a surprisingly variety of characteristics can be found among the vegetal and animal species both on the land and in the sea.

LAND VEGETAL SPECIES

Wild Mediterranean flora is relatively poor; there are few indigenous species. Indeed, almost all wild plants are natives of either Eurasia or Africa. Omnipresent bushes and shrubs are typical of the distinctive Mediterranean xeric vegetation, called *matorral* in Spanish. Botanists distinguish three milieus: first, where carob and olive trees coexist, secondly, the Mediterranean milieu and lastly the mountain milieu. The first consists of the warmest regions protected from wind and winter frost: southern Spain, Malta, Cyprus and the littoral periphery of North Africa and Egypt where spurges, locust trees, myrrh, jujube, oleanders and palm trees abound. The Mediterranean environment is that of both the olive tree and the mastic tree, known as the *maquis* and the *garrigues* or *phryganes* in Greece. Mastic trees, cane-apples, ferns, junipers, box trees, evergreen oaks, cork oaks, pines, not to mention thyme, lavender, rosemary and other sarsaparilla are widespread at altitudes between 100 and 700 meters, particularly on the northern shore of the Mediterranean.

The mountain milieu begins above 800 meters in altitude and is subject to cold wet winters. Here firs, tall pine, deciduous trees such as oaks, ashes and chestnut trees and steppes covered in graminaceae predominate. Authentic Mediterranean cultivated flora is hardly richer than its wild counterpart. Since ancient Greece, agriculture has been based on the same trilogy: olive trees, grapes and wheat. Nearly all the other species grown here, even the most familiar ones, came from afar. Many travelers perusing the northern Mediterranean countryside are unaware that before the arrival of the Arabs such vegetables and fruits as the lemon, orange, tangerine, plum, cucumber, melon, watermelon, artichoke, lettuce, cauliflower, beet and celery that abound in our markets were unknown! How many of us know that the different varieties of cacti, agaves, aloes and prickly pears came from the Americas? Or that the omnipresent eucalyptus is of Australian origin? That the cypresses that give such rhythm to the superb landscapes of Provence, Campania and Attica are Persian? That tomatoes are Peruvian, corn, beans and potatoes Mexican, pimentos from Guyana, rice from Asia, eggplants from India and peach trees from Iran?

Gazing upon the cornucopia of agricultural produce, one must remember that it is not nature which bestowed all this wealth on Mediterranean man. It is the result of his own patient work, tenacity and deep-rooted need for travel and exchanges.

Land animals

The story of the animals is quite different. The various species living on the surface of the earth were hardly affected when the African and Eurasian continents joined around 25 million years ago. The animals of these two parts of the world came into contact for the first time. Then began the slow process of cohabiting and cross-breeding which is at the origin of all contemporary species of the Mediterranean region, from rats to horses, and including birds and snakes. There were numerous bilateral exchanges. Antelopes and horses crossed over to Africa, while monkeys and elephants went in a northerly direction. Paleozoology has revealed some startling discoveries. Each time the water level rose in the Mediterranean, animals from either Africa or Eurasia found themselves prisoners on recently formed islands.

According to an interesting but contested hypothesis, rapid and sometimes surprising mutations took place as these animals adapted to their new natural surroundings. Certain large animals are thought to have become quite small, while others that originally were little grew at a surprising rate. The remains of pygmy elephants and hippopotami, as well as the skeletons of dwarf deer, were found in Sicily, Malta, Cyprus and several Aegean Islands. On the contrary, fossilized remains of giant rodents, shrew mice, dormice and porcupines were found in the Balearic Islands, Corsica, Sardinia and on the Calabrian coast which was formerly isolated by water. None of these species exist today, yet their vestiges are vital in understanding what took place in the Mediterranean area.

Chestnuts, long a dietary staple in southern France and Corsica, are gathered in August in the southern Cevennes.
The Romans are believed to have carried the chestnut tree
to other parts of the western Mediterranean.

◁ A lavender field in the foothills of the Luberon in Provence, France. This aromatic plant blooms in July and August
and produces a strongly scented, greatly appreciated essential oil.

The widely grown ivy-leafed geranium
or trailing pelargonium with its heavily
scented flowers.

The passion-flower is a tropical plant
that has adapted well to the
Mediterranean climate.
Its name refers to the shape
of the flower, which recalls the crown
of thorns, nails and hammers present
at the Passion of Jesus.

The laurel, symbol of victory
for the ancients, is a common
Mediterranean bush.

A bouquet of dates. Date palms
require a hot climate and can be found
in southern Spain, the Middle East
and along the African coast.

A green lizard
("lacerta trilineata"),
one of the many Lacertilia abounding
on the Greek island of Sifnos.

Cicadas are everywhere in the
Mediterranean region, living on trees
whose sap they suck emitting
stridently piercing sounds.

During the summer mating season
multitudes of butterflies
congregatein the valley of Petaloudes,
Rhodes.

Most of the animals that live on the neighboring continents can be found around the Mediterranean. A few have disappeared only recently. In the early years of the Christian era, lions haunted the Greek mountains, and even at the beginning of the twentieth century they were still hunted in North Africa. Zoology recognizes as indigenous those species that adapted a long time ago and developed new phenotypes in their new environment.

Some examples are the macaque in Algeria, Morocco and Gibraltar, the genet civet in Tuscany, Sardinia and Crete, various rodents, along the African and Middle Eastern shores, such as gerbils, jerboas, palm squirrels, hamsters, marbled ducks, warblers, swifts, varanian lizards in Algeria and Asia Minor, the Hermann tortoise, the asp and cerastes of North Africa, the chameleon of southern Spain and the ashy lizard of North Africa and Spain.

Sheep and goats are especially well adapted to the Mediterranean environment.
They require little food and since ancient times have provided the local populations with milk and meat.

For migratory birds, such as the pink flamingo,
Mediterranean countries (here, southern Spain)
are an ideal summer haven.

One of the hundreds of species of waders
to be found in the Mediterranean.

A male mallard,
a common variety in the Mediterranean basin.

A superb tursiop, one of the three varieties of dolphins that live in Mediterranean waters.
The others are the common dolphin and the blue and white dolphin.

SUBMARINE LIFE

What took place below the surface of the sea was quite different from the phenomena of terrestrial evolution. Paleontology and geology have noted that no form of life, whether vegetal or animal, was able to survive the drying up of the primitive sea and the over-salinization of the residual lakes. It is therefore impossible to find any species existent before seven million years ago. Only their fossil remains reveal what the first inhabitants of the Mediterranean waters were like. They were, for the most part, tropical species with Indo-Pacific affinities. The second observation follows from the first. Most of today's animal and vegetal species come from the Atlantic, which filled the Mediterranean depression for the last time around 6 million years ago. Biogeographers identify three groups. First, the authentic Atlantic species, representing 75% of marine life; second, the species called indigenous because, although originally from the Atlantic, they have adapted perfectly to their new environment and have since developed certain purely Mediterranean characteristics. They represent 20% of marine life. The last group of 5%, includes species that came from the Indian Ocean and the Red Sea via the Suez Canal and therefore known as "Lessepsians."

The first category includes a great number of fish, such as the diverse varieties of tunas, particularly red tunas, bonitos, bass, anglers, anchovies, mackerels and John Dorys, that can also be found in the Atlantic. Other less spectacular Mediterranean species live anywhere from 600 to 800 meters higher than their oceanic counterparts. Mediterranean water is generally 10°C warmer than Atlantic water at the same depth, for instance 13° instead of 3°C at depths of 200 to 300 meters. Most indigenous species came from the Atlantic, but mutated to their new environment ages ago, generating new original features. Groupers, soles, scorpion fish, wrasse, breams, mullets are some of the most well known.

Yet, the proportion of indigenous species within a given marine population may vary greatly. Thus, 45% to 50% of sponges and ascidia whose larva have a short life span and a limited dispersal area are indigenous, while only 18% of the decapodalous crustaceans whose larva live longer and which are more widely dispersed in the water are indigenous. Certain indigenous species even come from the Indo-Pacific area. Their presence in the Mediterranean raises still unanswered questions about how and when they arrived. The posidonia, for example, which are widespread in the Mediterranean, are also found in Australia, but never in the Atlantic. Some scientists see them as the descendants of the old tropical population of Thetys. However, given our present state of knowledge, it is impossible to imagine that a living species was able to survive the Tertiary cataclysm.

The "Lessepsians," for example, barracudas, rabbitfish and lizardfish, have come from the Red Sea since the opening of the Suez Canal in 1869. Certain zones of the eastern Mediterranean are experiencing a veritable colonization by fauna from the Red Sea. Studies have shown that both seas contemporaneously underwent identical phenomena of drying up; later they were also simultaneously filled and repopulated. However, while the Mediterranean was nourished by Atlantic wildlife, the Red Sea replenished its flora and fauna from the Indo-Pacific Ocean. Thus, the latter contains coral reefs unknown in the Mediterranean. When communication was established via the Suez Canal, these Indo-Pacific species migrated to the Mediterranean, although water temperatures there have prevented many of them from surviving. Constructor corals, for instance, require temperatures above 19°C. Others, however, have adapted. Ninety-six per cent cohabit in perfect harmony with the indigenous species, but some of the new arrivals, or "invaders" as marine ecologists call them, such as the Rhodilema nomadica, an enormous jellyfish, may be a threat to Mediterranean populations.

The polyprion or stonebass, a common Mediterranean fish, is a close relative of the grouper and prefers finding shelter within wrecked ships.

Arborescent red corals on a reef off the Isle of Capri.

*In the western Mediterranean,
a scorpion fish
on a mixed sea floor of rocks,
chalky algae and sponges.*

*The chromis
or mademoisel fish lives close
to its rocky hunting ground.*

◁

*Detail of a coral,
a colony of tiny animals
known as polyps
that live on microscopic animals
they catch with their tentacles.*

*The "airy" fineness
of the Sabella, a tube worm
that feeds on microorganisms.*

3

R. Campana

MEDITERRANEAN LANDSCAPES

Popular imagery has catalogued the Mediterranean basin as a vacation paradise, boasting of 3,000 hours of sun annually, a perfect azure sky, warm blue waters, white sand beaches, picturesque villages and characteristic cooking: a paradise where life is worth living and enjoying. No wonder each year, one-third of the world's tourists come seeking their "Eden" along the shores of the Mediterranean. Yet, few of the passing vacationers bother to take the time to look at and listen to the Mediterranean world. If they were but to leave the beaten path they would discover the true beauty of landscapes that are as violent as they are untamed and mysterious.

The bay of Almiros on the Cretan coast west of Rethimnon.

The deep creeks of Piana, on the western coast of Corsica are among the island's most spectacular pristine landscapes. ▷

STERN BEAUTY

Geographers consider the Mediterranean area to be one of the Earth's most perturbed.
As we have seen, the African and Eurasian lithospheric plates come together violently, causing brutal tellurian
phenomena. Earthquakes are frequent; there are numerous active volcanoes, and underwater,
the seafloor is sustaining intense pressure and uplifting. Both shores of the sea bear the marks of these colossal
upheavals which, little by little, have given the Mediterranean perimeter its present features.
Almost everywhere along the coast, mountains, with their scraggy relief, their chaotic scree, their slopes adorned
with colorful splashes of flowers can be seen reflected in the blue waters of the sea.

THE CIRCLE OF MOUNTAINS

Seen through the eye of a camera aboard a satellite, the Mediterranean resembles a small interior sea surrounded by an uninterrupted succession of massive mountains, although to the south it is bounded by nearly 2,000 kilometers of desert. This image of a circle of mountains is all the more surprising, for as one follows the shoreline along the narrow border of the Mediterranean's coastal plains, one does not have the impression that it is hemmed in by impressive heights. Yet, the mountains are there! Moreover, what mountains they are! Considering that certain submarine canyons descend over 4,000 meters below the sea and that the average height of the Mediterranean mountain faces are between 1,500 and 2,000 meters in altitude, there is a total variation in altitude of 7,000 or 7,5000 meters, honorable rivals for the prestigious summits of the Himalayas! Everywhere massive blocks of mountains of unequal heights seem to encroach upon the sea, in some places creating narrow cliff-framed straits - Gibraltar, Bonifacio or Messina, for example - in others, coastal ranges - the southern Alps, the Apennines, the Abruzzi, the Dinaric Alps, the Balkans, the Taurus, the Lebanon, the Atlas, the Pyrenees and the Betics - and in still others, the "last-born" long central backbone stretching from Sicily to Cyprus and crossing Malta and Crete. These mountain ranges provide the Mediterranean with its true framework; subdividing it into several secondary seas: the Alboran, the Ligurian, the Tyrrhenian, the Adriatic, the Ionian and the Aegean, plus the Sea of Marmara. With the exception of certain older crystalline massifs located in Provence and on the African shore of the Mediterranean, all the mountains that encircle the sea are high young sheer formations. The earliest uplift began around 60 million years ago when the first thrusts of the African plate encountered the Eurasian plate. Identical orogenises have resulted in identical physical features throughout the Mediterranean basin. Pointed peaks dominate the rough relief that has yet to be eroded by the weather. Deep fertile valleys are oriented towards the sea. Everywhere the rocky coastline is jagged and deeply indented. Uniformity, however, is not the rule. At times, the mountains disappear, yielding to vast flat open country; the sea washes the desert shoreline in the Middle Eastern and Africa, from southern Lebanon through Israel, Egypt and Libya to Tunisia. Likewise, on the north shore, the Rhone delta and the Po valley form wide coastal plains that perforate the circle of mountains. The conjunction of mountains, valleys, deserts and the sea offer a series of surprisingly varied landscapes that are, without exception, superb and sumptuous. Few places on earth can rival this beauty.

In the Balearic Islands the Puig Major range ends in high cliffs that drop into the sea, as here, south of Estallenchs.

In the early morning fog, the ghostly silhouettes of the Meteora rise above the Kalambaka plain.

The rock of Gilbratar has been an English possession in Spanish territory since 1713. It is one of the two ancient "Pillars of Hercules"; the other the Rock of Ceuta, faces it on the Moroccan coast.

This secluded spot on the gulf of Finike, Turkey, is a typical Mediterranean landscape, with garrigues and pine forests descending to the sea.

The spectacular 3,400 meter Sierra Nevada range that dominates the Grenada plain remains snowcapped most of the year.

The southern foothills of Cappadocia in Turkey are exceptional.
Water and wind erosion have carved out unusual shapes in the old tuff plateaus.

Except for the Maghrib ranges, the mountains on the southern shore of the Mediterranean Sea are relatively low
with eroded tabular reliefs such as the Jabal al Akhdar or the "Green Mountain" in Libya.

One of the many explosions of Etna whose on-going activity
is attested to by its unpredictable, violent "temper tantrums."
Its 3,345-meter summit is snowcapped for much of the year.

THE MAGIC OF VOLCANOES

Volcanoes are the most obvious proof of the earth's activity. They are merely the "mouths" through which subterranean fire is exhaled. From time immemorial eruptions have terrorized and fascinated mankind, accompanied as they often are by earthquakes. There ins no lack of volcanoes in the Mediterranean, from the still active Sicilian Etna to the extinct Turkish Hasan Dagi. The most famous among them is Vesuvius which in 79 AD destroyed the Roman cities of Herculaneum, Pompeii and Stabiae. Its 1,277-meter-high cone towers over the plain of Naples. The great southern Italian metropolis is only eight kilometers away, at the mercy of another of the giant's fits of anger. For the time being it is slumbering, but like all the other Mediterranean volcanoes it remains active, which means that some day, soon on the earth's time scale, it will awaken again.

Farther south, two other volcanoes in the Sicilian zone, Stromboli and Etna, often remind the local populations of their presence. Stromboli is the northeasternmost point of the Eolian or Lipari Islands, a volcanic archipelago. Night and day, it belches out a thick flume of smoke while its entrails emit muffled rumblings. Vulcano, another of the Eolians, is supposed to be home to the legendary Eole, the ancient god of the winds. It is closest to the Sicilian coast and is formed by three volcanic cones reaching a height of 500 meters. Lastly, in the northeastern part of the large island rises the majestic Etna. Its 3,345-meter summit is snowcapped for eight months of the year and it has never stopped spitting forth lava and volcanic slag.

The southernmost Greek island in the Cyclades, Santorin or Thera, is even more exceptional and can boast of a dramatic past. It is one of the most spectacular spots of the Mediterranean. The island looks like an enormous volcano whose center collapsed after a violent explosion and which was then invaded by the sea. Santorin has never been at rest.

During the Primary Era, it was part of the Aegean continent. During the great geological upheavals of the late Tertiary Era, it collapsed and the summits of the former mountains became islands, witnesses of the past. The two main mountains of Santorin, Profitis Ilian and Messa Vouno, date back to that period. It was, however, during the Quaternary that the island then located above a hot part of the lithosphere, took on its present appearance. Constant spectacular underwater eruptions gave it both its circular shape and its ancient Greek name, *Spongyla* or "the round." Seismic activity has continued nonstop. The villages of the island are regularly victims of convulsions, such as the 1956 quake that destroyed 2,000 homes and killed over fifty people. Of all the catastrophes that took place in ancient times, Santorin's is remembered best. Around 1530 BC Santorin literally exploded, forming an immense central crater, the present-day caldera, which was immediately invaded by waters rushing through the breach opened in the southwest. A thick cloud of ashes buried the opulent city of Akrotiri and other towns whose brilliant civilization flourished there. At the same time, the eruption created an enormous tidal wave that flooded Crete. This event may have been the basis of the famous legend of the Atlantis over which so much ink has been spilt and so many explorers' curiosity whetted since Plato first mentioned it in the fourth century BC.

The Santorin caldera.
The central crater, now invaded by the sea,
came into existence
during the volcanic eruption of 1530 BC
which destroyed the original island,
destroying contemporary Minoen palaces.

The sides of Vesuvius are covered by long gray cooled lava flows.
The new soil is fertile and new vegetation grows rapidly.

During the first century AD, the Pouzzoles sulfur springs,
the Romans' largest spa, were already famous for curing rheumatism.

These salt marshes in the bay of Ramla,
in the northern part of the island of Gozo have been exploited since prehistoric times.

Many salt troughs located below sea level ▷
can be seen along the desert plateau on the Egyptian Libyan border.

A LOVE STORY OF THE SEA AND THE WIND

The wind is what gives life to the waters of the Mediterranean. Without the wind it would be practically motionless. What is more beautiful than the choppy surface of the sea, with white foam carried from the blue-crested waves by the breath of violent squalls?
Wind is impalpable and invisible and yet it makes its existence felt so clearly.
The absence or presence of wind modifies both nature and man's character.
For ages, winds were thought to be emanations of friendly or evil gods
depending on whether they brought rejuvenating rain or destructive tempests.
Today they are the subject of meticulous scientific studies and have lost their mystery.

THE "MIRACLES" OF WATER, SALT AND WIND

The survival of life on earth has always been conditioned by the presence of water. The planet's first living organisms came into existence in water. Later, aquatic animals left the marine world for terra firma where mutations took place and new land species were born. To survive, these land animals needed fresh water. Thus, the miraculous system of water that allows creatures to live and to adapt came to exist. Humid air, after losing its salt, rises and cools in contact with the upper strata of the atmosphere above oceans and seas. This cooling process causes the condensation of water vapor into tiny drops that gather to form clouds that winds then drive above zones with rapidly changing climatic conditions (warm seas, mountains, valleys and lakes) where they grow bigger. When the drops of water are heavy and more numerous and can no longer remain in suspension, they fall to earth as rain, thus replenishing rivers and underground reserves with fresh water. River water then runs into the sea where its salt content increases, until once again it evaporates and a new cycle begins. The interaction of water and wind does not only take place on the land. The renewal of seawater is also closely linked to the wind pattern. The Mediterranean Sea is a typical example. Like all environments harboring living beings, the Mediterranean must, in order to stay alive, be regenerated both on the surface and in depth. The many winds blowing on its surface move colossal masses of water forward, causing a total renewal of the upper layers approximately every 90 years. As for the deeper waters, the determining influence of the winds is even more obvious. Indeed, the lighter, warmer upper layers hold down the dense and relatively cold deeper layers. For them to be replaced by "newer" waters they must rise to the surface. This can only happen during violent winter storms when the north wind blasts, raising and pushing the enormous liquid mass towards the south. It takes nearly 250 years for the complete vertical stirring to be achieved.

The magnificent one-hundred-meter high natural basins in Pamukkale,
western Turkey, are unique in the world.
They are supplied by the permanent flow of 45°C water rich in mineral salts.

The superb Sicilian Bay of Tindari,   ▷
sheltered by the cape cliffs of the same name, provides a completely wind free anchorage.

Along the northern coast of Egypt are lagoons, separated from the sea by sandbanks,
where good quality salt has been extracted since early ancient times.

One of the more visible effects of the many winds that sweep over the Mediterranean.

The salt marshes of Trapani, western Sicily. Windmills pump water through narrow canals.

THE MYSTERIES OF THE HEAVENS

Although for thousands of years, mankind speculated in vain about the winds and their strange paths across the sky, today new scientific technology is providing precise answers. The atmosphere is composed of a number of large more or less homogeneous air masses separated by atmospheric fronts. In each hemisphere there are tropical and polar air masses, subdivided into maritime air and continental air that move across the surface of the earth. Wind is simply air in motion. It moves according to three basic phenomena: atmospheric pressure, gravity and the rotation of the earth. There is also a strong relation between the latter and the distribution of solar energy on the surface of the planet. Air density variations, or the atmospheric pressure gradient, are due to differences in temperature between the warm air of equatorial regions and the cold air of polar zones. Winds function by transporting hot air masses northward and southward to compensate for the constant heat deficit at the two poles. At the same time, the thermal imbalance between the different zones is perpetuated by radiation of the sun. As the winds are never able to compensate for the heat deficit, they continue relentlessly their round above the earth. The effect of the rotation of the earth on air currents is now also understood. These currents deviate towards the left in the Southern Hemisphere and towards the right in the Northern Hemisphere, where the Mediterranean is located. This phenomenon of deviation, which is observed on bodies in movement at the surface of the earth and in the atmosphere, is known as the "Coriolis force," named for the French scientist

who discovered it early in the nineteenth century. Whereas in equatorial and tropical regions, this force is quite attenuated and winds blow air masses from high pressures toward low pressures, in temperate and polar regions the opposite takes place. The strength of the Coriolis force determines the geostrophic winds, or those parallel to isobars, curves that join together areas of the earth where atmospheric pressure is identical. It follows that in the northern hemisphere, air masses carried by the winds turn in a clockwise direction around anticyclones and counter-clockwise around depressions. This is confirmed by the numerous popular sayings in the Mediterranean area recounting that rain comes from the south and the west and good weather from the north and east. Certain isolated regions are exceptions to the rule, for instance Provence where bad weather comes from the east as a result of the circular movement of winds over the southern Alps. In the Mediterranean area, the dominant west-east airflow is often unstable, producing alternating depressions and anticyclones. At high altitudes, temperature differences between the continents and the seas disturb the airflow, as do differences in atmospheric pressure between the plains and the highlands. A last remark needs to be made about breezes and local winds. The former originate in coastal areas and near lakes; they are quite frequent in the Mediterranean region and contribute to the charm of its climate. During the day, the rays of the sun heat the air above the land. It rises, and if it is laden with humidity, creates clouds. Little by little, cooler air from the sea replaces it. This movement is known as a sea breeze. The nighttime cooling of the earth induces the opposite phenomenon. Local winds, on the other hand, are closely linked to terrain features. They may accelerate greatly as they pass through a gap between two mountains, as do the *mistral* and the *tramontane*. They may also become warmer and drier after

The flourmills on Mykonos are inactive today,
but remain one of the most widely photographed sites of the Cyclades.

bringing rain to a mountainside, like the *foehn*, when it descends on the other face. In ancient times, however, this information was unknown. It is therefore not surprising that the ancients made divinities of the winds, those natural forces inhabiting the high ethereal realms of the sky and whose mechanisms escaped them.

SACRED WINDS AND EXISTING WINDS

The Mediterranean peoples gave human faces to the winds that alternately aided and terrorized them. Seth of the Egyptians, Enlil the master wind of the Sumerians, Baal the storm god of the Phoenicians and Hadad, his Aramean counterpart, are just a few of the distant ancestors of Aeolus, venerated by the Greeks and Romans as the great master of the winds. Aeolus's realm was the Mediterranean and he was the subject of innumerable legends. The ancient Greeks localized certain of his palaces in the Aegean Islands, but believed that his favorite home was further west in the Aeolian islands, on Vulcano. For these communities of navigators,

Aeolus was the most important god of nature, and the most formidable, to say the least. Angry, he could call up the most terrible storms, but once calmed, his breath allowed them to navigate rapidly to distant destinations. Most of the ancient winds were related to Aeolus. Their names were *Apheliotes, Aquilon, Notos or Auster, Boreas or Septentrion, Kekias or Koekras, Euros, Lips, Sciron, Yapix or Circlus and Zephyr or Favonius*. Each blew from a precise point on the horizon and the navigator's skill allowed him to use them to his best advantage. Little has changed since then. The privileged, some might call it "mystical", relationship between

Mediterranean man, nature and the wind still exists. Names have changed, but the day by day reality is identical. When a Mediterranean farmer rises, he always scans the sky and sniffs the wind to know what kind of a day it will be.

The fisherman "smells" if the sea will be too rough for him to embark or if, on the contrary, the winds are favorable.

Whether he is Christian, Muslim or atheist makes no difference; before leaving he will make a little gesture to the sea and to the wind. The Sicilian or Cypriot will throw a few flowers in the air or on the surface of the waves. Maltese and Greek ships have eyes painted or carved on their prows, while Tunisian and Lebanese boats have little niches for offerings arranged under the gunwale. On terra firma both the southern Italian and the Turkish farmer will deposit a few seeds or a vial of olive oil at the foot of the oldest tree or on a tiny altar built in the middle of his fields.

The names of the winds vary from place to place in the Mediterranean region; quoting all of them would be most tiresome. The same wind may have a different name at a distance of only a few dozen kilometers. Several winds blow over the same region. There are over two hundred winds in French Provence alone! Among the land winds there is the *tramontane*, which is a northerly, the *mistral* rushing down from the northwest, the *ponant* coming out of the west, that correspond respectively to the ancient *Boreas*, *Apix* and *Zephyr*. There are also numerous sea winds, including the *levant*, from the east, the *sirocco* from the south and the *largade* a westerly from the sea. Certain "great" Mediterranean winds are well known to everyone.

The geographic features of the western portion of the area, such as the height of the mountains, the existence of large islands and the proximity of the African and European

There are more windmills in the Balearic Islands than elsewhere in the western Mediterranean.
They are still widely used in Mallorca. This mill is near Son Ferriol.

continents, cause the air to be more 'tormented' here and therefore there are more winds. As one moves eastward, they are fewer in number. In the western basin, proceeding eastward one encounters first the cold, wet easterly *levant*, then the humid westerly *poniente* which affects the Alboran Sea, southern Spain and northern Morocco, next, the *vendavales* from Africa and the westerly *garbi* which blows over eastern Spain and the Gulf of Lion. There are also the *tramontane* from the northwest and the *autan* from the southwest, both of which crisscross over lower Languedoc, followed by the violent *mistral* which is cold and dry and clears the southern French skies. Then comes the monsoon-like southeasterly *marin*, often considered the mistral's antagonist, then the cold dry *tramontana* that blows off the Italian Alps, the warm humid easterly *bentu de soli*, that affects Sardinia, the southwesterly *libeccio* and its opposite the

northeasterly *gregal* whose regions are Italy and Corsica and finally the warm humid *sirocco* born in the desert zones of North Africa. The eastern Mediterranean basin is the center for "simpler" winds that fall either into the cold wind or warm wind category. Among the former are the *gregale*, a violent cold dry wind from the northeast, the glacial northern *vandarac* that freezes Macedonia in winter, the mild easterlies, *antolikos* and *apeliotes*, the northeasterly *meltem*, which is even colder and more violent than the *mistral* and which disturbs summertime navigation. All of them blow in the Aegean and Ionian region. The *sirocco* is a southerly. Further east are the *bora* and the *revolin*, two cold winds coming from the northeast that dominate in the vast region from the Black Sea to the Adriatic. The areas of the southeast and the far-eastern Mediterranean often experience hot dusty desert winds such as the *khamsin*.

The Roman agora in Athens. In the background the famous hexagonal wind? tower in Attica, built by the Romans during the first century. It accommodated Andronicus Kyrristos's water clock.

The Maltese coast. In the Mediterranean when the winds reach force 7,
as they frequently do, small craft can no longer navigate on the raging sea.

A small Greek Orthodox chapel typical of the Cyclades. ▷
The three basic colors, red, white and blue, are traditional.

WILD SECRETS

Anyone who has spent some time on the Mediterranean coast knows that it is one of the most beautiful regions on earth, and one of the most crowded. In addition to the roughly 200 million native Mediterraneans living along the coast and in the backcountry, there are nearly 110 million tourists yearly that throng to its beaches and swim in its waters between the months of June and September. Has the Mediterranean then become a place to be avoided? Has it lost the magical beauty that for millennia has attracted and enchanted generations of visitors? Today, if one wishes to enjoy the Mediterranean of the past, one must seek it in the rural countryside, shunning the large urban centers.

REBELLIOUS NATURE

The stereotyped image of eternal leisure found in the holiday brochures must be forgotten. Mediterranean lands are arid and harsh on the people who inhabit them. As seen from Paris, Rome, Athens or Cairo, the "Med" has a reputation for vacationing and *dolce farniente*. This is the seductive impression of city dwellers staying in the luxury hotels along the coast and relaxing on the golden sandy beaches, who do not live there full time. Often they look condescendingly down on the local inhabitants as if they were lazy loafers who have nothing to do but drink pastis or ouzos on café terraces and play petanque or cricket in the shade of the olive trees. They seem to think that the local motto is "how pleasant to be in the shade idling the time away." In fact, they have no idea how hard farming rocky fields on steep hillsides is nor how parsimonious the sea can be with fishermen out in their boats until dawn. In spite of magnificent countrysides, unusually bright skies and a clement climate, the region is not paradise on earth. The soil is often friable and poor, except in the estuaries and lands that receive river deposits. When rainfall is slight, the earth is literally burnt, and only the scant scrub vegetation of the *maquis* and *garrigue* grows. If rainfall is too abundant, topsoil slides down mountain slopes and obstructs

rivers, which in turn overrun their banks causing tremendous floods. Over the past few years, France, northern Italy, Turkey and Morocco have had this experience. Only man's tenacity and intelligence have allowed him to master natural forces at their superb and rebellious best. Man's first task was to find fresh water, the most precious of resources in the Mediterranean region. Then it had to be canalized to irrigate fields. Septic zones had to be drained, in particular marshes rampant with miasma and malaria. Only then could man cultivate the meager soil and, by the sweat of his brow, bring it to bear fruit. Over the course of centuries, this exacting labor often had to be started afresh, as the forces of nature, refusing to be tamed, undid what man had so painstakingly done. The successive generations of Mediterranean dwellers have never been able to slacken their daily efforts. Indeed, if for some reason man fails to keep a watchful eye on the forces of nature, controlling and regulating them, they will, at the first opportunity, reassert their hold. Witness the dramatic consequences of rural exoduses, unfortunately so commonplace in the backcountry. First brambles and bushes invade the abandoned rooms and gardens, and then roofs collapse and walls fall to ruin. Even the patiently constructed terraces that climb up the mountainside tumble down. Marshes invade formerly cultivated plains and scrub brush covers paths.

The "Paradise Coast" near Puerto Leccio in northwestern Sardinia: the delight of pristine nature as yet unspoiled.

Procuring arable plots from unamenable land has not been easy.
Men have constructed terraces for orchards and olive groves, as in Vouni, Cyprus, ▷
and for vineyards, as in Monolithos in Greece.

Fishing boats have already been pulled onto the beach,
as the sunset tints the walls of the fortified port of Hammamet in Tunisia.

Located at the foot of an imposing rocky headland on the Tyrrhenian coast of Sicily is the picturesque village of Cefalu, a site that has been inhabited since the ninth century BC.

HIDDEN CHARMS

It is, however, this very wildness that gives the region its charm. The combination of trees and stones, and plants and dust, create a disquieting feeling in visitors. The stifling heat of the sun on calm days, make one light-headed. The crickets' strident song seems to pierce one's eardrums, thorny bushes scratch one's skin as sharp stones roll away underfoot. Everything appears aggressive, yet there is something both magical and appealing in the aggression. This is the realm of rough untamed beauty. The earth is red, then without warning becomes white. Huge rocky blocks rise in fantastic violet, brown or ochre forms cutting off the horizon. Suddenly one comes upon a tiny forgotten vale with green thickets growing along the banks of a dry brook. The myriad colors of Mediterranean flowers, whether indigenous or not, brighten the thick, impenetrable brushwood. Here one stumbles upon a bouquet of pink and red bougainvillea, elsewhere, a bed of white, pink or mauve nimble fingers, or again some yellow

laburnum, or convolvulus with their deep blue corollas, and white or pale pink cistus. Further along are rows of prickly pear trees topped by small yellow flowers, the elegant blood-red corollas of the hibiscus or the pinkish and mauve boughs of the Judas tree swaying in the wind.

As one approaches the shoreline, the Mediterranean countryside reveals its ultimate secrets, like valuable jewels reserved for the sea: thousands of coves, bights, bays and creeks nestled in the bosom of red, gold or gray rock barriers. They abound in Corsica, Sardinia, Malta, Sicily, Cyprus, and along the Spanish, French, Peloponnessian, Turkish and Syrian coasts. Even busy tourist areas such as the central Cyclades and Mallorca conceal still others, yet unknown to the public. Finding them may require much searching far off the beaten path. Clearly, most of the streams have already been influenced by man and transformed into small ports or marinas. The few remaining can only be reached from the sea or after a long

hike. Indeed, it is still possible to discover one's dream cove on the Mediterranean, where hectic mass tourism with its need for modernity is out of place and where true nature lovers can communicate with the original Mediterranean environment.

Those who have a taste for discovery, those who take the time to seek, look and listen will always find their "secret" spot to enjoy undisturbed. There, the sky will truly be bluer, the air purer and the land and the sea more beautiful.

◁ *The Sainte Baume, a limestone massif whose summit attains 1,147 meters, accommodates one of the most important places of pilgrimage in Provence, the monastery of Sainte Marie-Madeleine.*

Set into the ochre-pink canyon wall at Wadi Qelt, the monastery of Saint George of Koziba, founded around 450 AD has withstood the tumultuous events of the past centuries.

A typical picture postcard view of the tourist's Mediterranean dream:
a shepherd and his flock of goats on the jagged Turkish coast with the deep blue sea in the background.

A Berber countrywoman walking among the broom on the flanks of the Moroccan Rif.

In the region of Massa Lubrense, the vineyards stretch down rocky slopes to the Gulf of Capri.

The beautiful villages of Braccolaccia and Farinole, west of Cap Corse,
are like jewels set in a casket of green mountains.   ▷

A shepherd from Chergui, one of the three Kerkennah Islands lying off the eastern coast of Tunisia.

The Sinai Desert ends in long orange dunes that stretch northwestward before becoming a narrow coastal belt in the region of Al Arish, Egypt.

The magnificent creek in the Marseilles-Veyre massif.
The calm turquoise waters attract pleasure boats and deep-sea divers.

In bad weather the Bay of Dwejra on the Maltese island of Gozo deserves its nickname of "Doorway to the sea."

A natural entrance canal between two white cliffs links the city of Bonifacio to the strait known as the "mouths" of Bonifacio that separates Corsica and Sardinia.

4

R. Campana

THE RICHEST HISTORY IN THE WORLD

The Mediterranean basin has seen the birth and death of more prestigious cultures than any other region of the world. The first great civilizations were born in the eastern part of the Mediterranean after the all=important Neolithic revolution when Middle Eastern man invented farming. All of them were primarily rural civilizations, contrary to a widespread but relatively recent idea linking them to the sea. While for many centuries urban dwellers and farmers were busy building large cities and creating complex irrigation systems to water arid lands, the sea remained desperately empty. Rafts and primitive canoes occasionally navigated along the coasts and around the islands, but until early antiquity, no regular maritime communication existed.

Just outside of Kato Zakro, Cyprus, is the architectural site known as "the royal tombs,"
a fourth-century BC Hellenistic necropolis with partially subterranean tombs carved into the rock.

Comparisons with the drawings and bas-reliefs of the ancient Egyptians
reveal that millennia later Nile Delta felucca have hardly changed. ▷

EARLY ANTIQUITY

At the beginning of the third millenium BC, it became apparent that Neolithic civilization was suffering from problems of transportation. This is when the major event known by certain historians as the "ship revolution" took place. As life styles became increasingly refined in the large cities of Mesopotamia and Lower Egypt, trade developed to meet the demand for foreign goods. New horizons rapidly became necessary. Only by using the rivers, and later, the seas would the development of large scale communication be possible. Small craft began to appear on three major rivers, the Tiger, the Euphrates and the Nile. Once their waterways were mastered, other better designed and sturdier craft set out to visit the Persian Gulf, the Red Sea and finally the Mediterranean coasts.

THE ADVENT OF SEA GOING SHIPS

The Egyptians and the Canaanites, ancestors of the future Phoenicians, were undoubtedly the first to sail the Mediterranean waters regularly. Trade between these two cultural and economic giants grew as Egypt came to require Lebanese cedars, Dead Sea bitumen and Syrian oil, whereas the peoples of the Lebanese-Syrian coast valued Egyptian granite, precious stones, gold and ivory. As the Neolithic period drew to a close, large trading fleets ensured permanent exchanges between the ports of Lower Egypt and those of the Canaan zone. At the same time, ceramic objects were already being produced in the small coastal towns of Cyprus and in northern Crete and ships were venturing further away to explore unknown shores.

In addition, during the third millennium BC, aided by the first broad cultural exchanges, there flourished the splendid but short-lived civilization of the Cyclades. In that circular Aegean archipelago, clans built cist tombs and produced remarkably delicate and well-designed handicrafts. Jewelry, statues and vases all reveal a unique sensitivity that was very closely linked to the sea, as can be seen by the omnipresence of ship patterns in their decorations. At approximately at the same time, in western Cyprus the inhabitants set up numerous Copper Age sites such as those in Lempa and Kisonerga, where a fecundity cult developed. Copper mining spread, bringing wealth to those city-states possessing the ore.

Much further to the west, surprising Stone Age civilizations characterized by important fecundity cults were also coming to life. People about whom we still know very little erected gigantic stone monuments in Corsica and the islands of Gozo and Malta. The Corsican site of Filitosa contains remarkable megalithic statuary. In Malta the remains are even more impressive, ranging from tombs dug into mountainsides nearly 5,000 years ago to the large temples and monumental underground burial chambers, such as Mnadjra, Hagar Kim and Ggantija, constructed 600 years later. Some, such as Hal Saflieni, built on several levels and containing 7,200 corpses, were quite vast. This Maltese site appears to have been the last place in the Mediterranean where large-scale fecundity cults existed.

The megalithic site of Filitosa in southern Corsica has been occupied for nearly eight thousand years.
It contains circular monuments and statue-menhirs carved and erected some four thousand years ago.

*Like the nuraghi, the "Giants Tombs" near Arzachena
are unique Sardinian funeral monuments.*

*The San Antine nuraghe is one of the most interesting in the valley of the nuraghi.
These Bronze Age monuments are generally truncated towers that undoubtedly served as refuges or fortresses.*

The prehistoric temples at Mnajdra and Hagar Qim in southern Malta are,
along with others of the same sort on the island, the oldest erected monuments in the world.
Radiocarbon tests have proved they were built over 5,000 years ago.

Egyptians and Cretans: the first high seas navigators

In the second millennium BC, Mediterranean navigation was characterized by the appearance of a new type of ship; it was lighter, but more importantly, it was sturdier due to the presence of a hull and keel. The Aegeans perfected the model, thus allowing their sailors, and then merchants, to venture out to sea and to resist the sudden, violent squalls. These progressively replaced the Levantine ships. Authentic trade multiplied cultural exchanges in the eastern part of the Mediterranean, while the western half remained under-developed. Many historians have concluded that the appearance of Aegean seamanship is the starting point of the first cosmopolitan Mediterranean civilization. Voyages, embassies, exchanging of gifts and diplomatic missions succeeded one another thanks to the sea going fleets.

Who were these Aegean innovators? They were early Greeks. Historians date their rise from the last third of the third millennium BC. Rich city-states, namely Zakros, Palaikastro,

Mochlos and Gournia located for the most part on the western coast of Crete, had begun by controlling the main trade routes in the central Mediterranean. At the beginning of the second millennium, at the time of Minoan II, all these cities had come under the yoke of the quasi-imperial power concentrated in the powerful city of Knossos. This is the period of the early palaces and the large two- or three-story houses typical of ancient Crete. Archeological discoveries have revealed the refined elegance and the sophistication of this society. Between 1700 and 1600 BC terrible earthquakes destroyed the proud metropolis and its satellite settlements. Yet, their wealth and development were such that in fewer than fifty years even more beautiful and majestic palaces and homes were rebuilt on the original sites. For the next three centuries, the Minoan civilization in Crete, named after the legendary King Minos of Knossos, spread its influence over the entire eastern half of the Mediterranean. The splendid ruins of

Knossos, Mallia, Phaïstos, Haghia Triada and Tylissos all attest to this golden age, the most exceptional cultural development the Mediterranean has ever known. All later civilizations were in one way or another to be its heirs. The following figures will give some idea of its splendor. The city of Knossos alone, located near present-day Iraklion, had a population of over 80,000 inhabitants, a colossal number for those times! The famous palace of Minos, where the legendary Minotaur was kept, was five stories high and had over 13 rooms. The interior comfort was such that water arrived in each room by means of a hydraulic system that only came to France in the 18th century.

The Egyptians were the first sailors to venture forth along the Mediterranean coast.
Their centuries of navigating on the Nile enabled them to build lighter sturdier ships
with large sails that could take to the sea.

◁ *The Sphinx, the supreme emblem of the divinity, best symbolizes the mystery of ancient Egypt.*

Despite the rather fanciful "reconstruction" of the Palace of Minos in Knossos by the English archeologist
Sir Arthur John Evans at the beginning of this century, visitors can understand how the several storied complicated network
of corridors and rooms gave birth to the myth of the Labyrinth.

The pipelines and huge jars kept in the Knossos storerooms testify to the sophisticated plumbing, heating,
water supply and food preservation systems the ancient Cretans devised.

One enters the Mycenaean fortress through the famous "Lion Gate."
This remarkable construction dates from the fifteenth and sixteenth centuries BC.

ACHAEAN INVASIONS

Unfortunately ill luck struck the Minoan civilization for the second time, destroying it definitively around 1450 BC, probably after an invasion by the Achaeans, Indo-Europeans that had infiltrated the Balkan Peninsula early in the second millennium. Crete, however, had had the time to export its brilliant model and lifestyle. Many Cretan colonies had been established in the Peloponnese, then later in continental Greece. Cretan influence was subsequently felt in the Cyclades and western Asia Minor, where the islands of Delos, Melos, Samos, Cos and Rhodes and towns such as Miletus were home to authentic Cretan settlements. The small Greek cities that had erected "Cretan palaces" at the beginning of the 16th century BC soon became capitals of separate rival kingdoms: Mycenae, Tyrinthe in the Peloponnese, Athens in Attica, Gla in Boeotia and

Iolkos in Thessaly are some of the most noteworthy. Smaller Cretan-type cities can also be found in the Lipari Islands and from Sicily to the Syrian coast. The objects unearthed in the rulers' great burial monuments, gold masks, stone-studded diadems, arms, armor, belts, jewels and war chariots, are rivaled only by the graves of Egyptian pharaohs.

In the 15th century BC, it was Mycenaean culture that expressed its originality by combining Achaean taste for the monumental with the Cretans' refined complexity. The most beautiful examples of Mycenaean talent were found in the city of Mycenae itself. The first authentic Greek writing came from there, a derivative of Linear B, the ancient disyllabic Cretan system. Numerous Minoan deities, such as Potnia, who became Artemis, were integrated into the most important positions in the

Achaean pantheon. This blending of cultures achieved its most successful results, however, in the realm of art, especially in architecture and statuary. The Achaeans then exported their culture throughout the Mediterranean area. As they were able to navigate everywhere, they became the first true Mediterranean sailors. Traces of their visits can be found in the west in Ischia and Taranto in continental Italy, on the Lipari islands and in Sicily, as well as further east in Troy and Miletus in Asia Minor, in the Cyclades and Cyprus, in Alalah in Cilicia, in Ugarit in Syria and in Byblos, Sidon and Tyr in Lebanon. Yet, in spite of its military power, the Mycenaean civilization collapsed suddenly around 1200 BC, probably after attacks by new invaders or as a result of popular revolts. For several centuries, the entire Greek world fell prey to obscurantism.

It fell to the Levant to carry the Mediterranean torch once again. All cultural and commercial exchanges between Mesopotamia, Egypt and the West had to pass the rich Syro-Palestinan region. Cypriots and Mycenaeans flocked to the large coastal cities where descendants of the Canaanites and oriental peoples lived side by side. To the south, Byblos became the vanguard of Mediterranean culture, while in the north the port of Minat al Baïda allowed Ugarit to monopolize trade. Ugarit reached the apex of its prosperity in the 14th and 13th centuries BC. The peaceful coexistence of worshipers in the great sanctuaries devoted to the major Oriental deities, Baal, Daga, An, Isis and Astarte, offers proof of its cosmopolitanism. Further evidence was the use of five systems of writing to transcribe the eight local languages. However, the capital's real stroke of genius was the invention of the world's first alphabet at the end of the 12th century BC.

A brief period of decline affected the great Levantine kingdoms, causing a sudden drop in maritime traffic.

The Achaean tombs (here, the Treasury of Atreus at Mycenae) are huge hypogea whose size and majesty reveal the builders' precision and taste for the monumental.

The political events in Lebanon have brought to a halt the archeological excavations of this superb site dedicated
to the Phoenician god Ashmoun. The central temple, built on a 60-meter by 44-meter rectangular plan, was destroyed by fire
in the fourth century BC by King Okhos in order to quell a revolt led by the inhabitants of Sidon.

THE PHOENICIAN AND GREEK GOLDEN AGES

*During the ninth century BC, the Phoenician and Greek cities established a new commercial and cultural revival
in the eastern Mediterranean. Within one century, they had recovered their former prosperity.
Next, they turned their eyes to the trading outposts further to the occident, bringing to this early "Far West"
an intense period of cultural and economic colonization. The westward movement followed three routes.
The northernmost, proceeded along the shores of present-day Turkey and Greece, as far as the island of Corfu.
The central route advanced along the chain of the mid-Mediterranean islands of Cyprus, Crete, Malta, Sicily,
Sardinia and the Balearic Islands. Finally, there was the southern route,
along the Egyptian, Libyan and North African coasts to Gibraltar.*

THE PHOENICIANS' RACE WESTWARD

The Phoenicians had already established dense settlements along the coast of present-day Lebanon, perfecting the accomplishments of their Canaanite predecessors. Indefatigable navigators, they carried on the oriental merchant tradition and were the first to set out towards the west, establishing trading outposts on the far side of the Mediterranean. Their enterprises flourished in Cyprus, Sicily, Sardinia, Africa and even in Spain. They could boast of having founded Carthage where the brilliant Punic civilization subsequently developed. From the ports of Tyr, Sidon and Byblos large round-bottomed ships sailed off with blacksmiths' and goldsmiths' goods, as well as loose woolen cloth and the famous dyes extracted from murex, a shell which, when ground, produced superb pinks, violets and purples. Phoenician domination of the Mediterranean lasted for nearly three centuries, before storm clouds gathered over the maritime power.

Competition from the Greeks became more pressing. The Assyrians, who had invaded Cyprus at the end of the 8th century BC, were already a constant threat to eastern maritime routes. Less than a century later, the Assyrians occupied Egypt, thus depriving Phoenician ports of a substantial part of their trading income. The Phoenicians were not a nation of warriors, but of merchants. As they were both realistic and pragmatic, they chose the only viable solution, to submit to the Assyrians' diktat in order to preserve what could be, rather than to engage in a fruitless battle. When powerful Assyria in turn fell to Babylon, the Phoenicians did not hesitate to pledge allegiance to the new masters. In doing so, they lost their cultural identity and were soon assimilated in a heterogeneous mass of what the Greeks condescendingly called the "eastern Barbarians." Now cut off from its "motherland," Carthage decided to act independently. It undertook an imperialistic venture and was, within a few centuries, at the height of its power.

General view showing the thirteen levels of the ancient city of Byblos, one of the oldest cities in the world.
The residential areas, streets and to the right, the fortifications, are clearly visible.
In the background, a few columns where the Roman agora was located.

One of the large underground tombs for kings and prominent people in Byblos.

ARCHAIC GREECE

In the 8th century BC the cities of continental Greece and Peloponnese imposed their cultural and commercial rule on the central and eastern Mediterranean, before beginning a timid march westward. The Greek world was just emerging from four centuries of obscurantism following the fall of the Mycenaean civilization. Hierarchical royal families governed small city-states. All Greeks, however, despite their continual rivalries and clashes were nevertheless aware that they belonged to the same people and spoke the same language. Even at the height of the fratricidal fighting among the powerful city-states, Greeks always felt a strong common feeling of superiority towards the mixed Barbarian populations. It is upon this elitist, even racist, attitude that Greek expansion in the Mediterranean was founded. In rapid succession, they extended their control over greater Greece, which included southern Italy and Sicily, Marseille, founded by the Phoceans in the sixth century BC, and much of Corsica, where Aleria was built. Simultaneously, their influence was to bear on the shores of the Hellespont and western Asia Minor (present-day Turkey). Taking advantage of its position of strength, Greece made military and trade alliances with the local powers, Lydia, Phyrgia and Lycia. On both shores of the Aegean Sea mixed marriages, commercial exchanges, reciprocal missions and artistic syncretism were the signs of the first Greek age. Moreover, "true "Greeks considered the inhabitants of Asia Minor as their eastern brothers.

The famous Delos lions carved in Naxos marble are the last witnesses of the Archaic culture that flourished in this part of the Cyclades seven centuries before the Common Era.

Greater Greece, however, was soon prey to violent invaders, the Cimmerians and the Scythes from Iran, then the Assyrians and subsequently, the Persians. The latter represented a highly sophisticated civilization and were possessed by a terrible yearning for conquest. It was unfortunately at this time, with the Persians threatening their eastern borders, that the principal Greek cities entered a phase of unremitting internecine rivalry. The first "holy war" was waged among the main Greek cities in 590 BC, causing the total destruction of the sanctuary in Delphi, which, symbolically signified the end of the collective Greek identity. Finally two cities emerged and took precedence over their rivals. Athens dominated continental Greece in the southeast and northern Peloponnese, while central and southern Peloponnese was under Spartan influence. Corinth and Thebes, two smaller cities, subtly attempted to take advantage of this nascent friction by playing off one against the other. This rivalry took place at the end of the 6th century BC when Greek trade in the Mediterranean had expanded considerably and had definitively supplanted that of the Phoenicians.

From 314 to 166 BC when Delos was independent of Athenian domination, its inhabitants built many monuments, such as this large theater overlooking the bay.

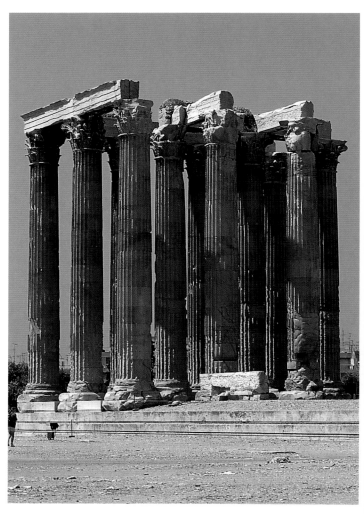

◁ The majestic acropolis in Lindos, Rhodes, dominates the bay whose reputation for safe anchorage dates back to ancient times.
The primitive foundations of the city are 35 centuries old.
During the Greek era a large sanctuary dedicated to Athena was built here.

Only fifteen of the original one hundred and four 17-meter-high columns of the prestigious temple dedicated to Olympian Zeus
remain standing. It took the Athenians five centuries, with the later aid of the Romans to complete the gigantic undertaking.

The Acropolis of Athens as seen from the Hill of the Muses. The Propylaea, the Erechteum, and the Parthenon,
the great temple to Athena, are also visible. At the foot of the rock is the Roman Odeum of Herodes Atticus.

The century of Pericles

Greek and especially Athenian ships dominated the Mediterranean world. Unexpectedly, new trouble was brewing in the east. In 494 BC the Persian king, Darius, sacked the city of Miletus in Asia Minor because this Ionian trade outlet had, with the help of Athens, revolted against the Persian king. After a long period of mutual observation and unofficial diplomacy, relations between Athens and Persia suddenly worsened. Four years after the fall of Miletus, the Persian flotilla was sent on an expedition against the Cyclades and Euboea, interrupting the profitable Aegean trade. Next, Persian troops debarked on the beaches of Marathon. It was there that the Athenians and the Plataeans, who had been abandoned by the Spartans on the pretext that it was during religious celebrations, beat back the Persian warriors in an overwhelming victory. The defeated Persian fleet retreated, ending the first of the Persian wars. For the next ten years Athens unilaterally ruled the cultural, political, economic and military world of the Mediterranean. It drew much of its wealth from the abundant lead and silver deposits that had been discovered on the sides of Mount Laurion and used this wealth to build the most powerful navy and the largest merchant marine ever.

The Persian sovereigns refused to abandon the profitable trade opportunities a Mediterranean outlet afforded and this eventually brought on the second Persian war. Once again Persian armies surged westward. In 480 BC, Xeres, Darius's son, was in his turn beaten by a coalition of Greek cities led by Athens and Sparta. The naval victory at Salamis was crucial to the outcome of the war. The Greeks, however, paid heavily for their victory. The Spartan elite was massacred, despite its determined resistance at the Thermopylae pass and Athens was burnt to the ground. Yet, an even stronger Athens emerged from the ashes. The city, indeed all of Greece, then entered the Golden Age or the century of Pericles, that illustrious strategist who led Athens for thirty years. Greek influence was so widespread that the term the "Greek miracle" is often used. Classical Greek artists produced some of mankind's most beautiful masterpieces: the Parthenon in Athens, the temple of Poseidon in Sounion, the tholos in Delphi and the sculptures of Phidias and Praxitel, to mention only a few.

Athenian preeminence throughout the Mediterranean area was incontestable. This hegemony triggered defiance among Athenian rivals, principally Sparta. The early conflicts soon came to a head in the violent fratricidal Peloponnesian War, which reduced Greece to ruin in less than a year. Sparta defeated Athens, but was so weakened that shortly thereafter Thebes was able to conquer it.

The most well known monument in Delphi, the holy city of Phocis, is the tholos.
This marble monument was built by the architect Theodoros in honor of the goddess Athena
during the first half of the fourth century BC.

Theban supremacy was short-lived. Philip II, sovereign of Macedonia, a northern kingdom, brought agreement among the Greek cities by vanquishing them all. In twelve short years, his son, Alexander the Great, accomplished the feat of building the largest empire ever known. After conquering his traditional enemy the Persians, he was unchallenged and imposed Greek influence throughout the Orient. The result was the extraordinary Hellenistic civilization, a hybrid of Greek genius and oriental culture that dominated the Mediterranean world and the Middle East. Because of their artistic brilliance and the vigor of their commerce, two cities predominated: Rhodes and later Alexandria, the Egyptian coastal city founded by the great conqueror.

This famous capital had a 180-meter-high lighthouse whose beacon guided vessels both day and night towards its storm-protected port. Hellenistic culture, however, presented some failings. The Macedonians lacked a seafaring tradition and inevitably neglected the Athenian trade empire. The Egyptians, on the other hand, now masters in the field of commerce, were incapable of modernizing their army. Therefore, despite the prestige associated with the Alexandrian epic and the cultural life of Rhodes and Alexandria, Greek dreams faded. Alexandrian splendor began to decline. By the time the great conqueror died in 323 BC the star of a new master, Rome, was ascending in the western Mediterranean.

The most beautiful Greek temples are found in Sicily and southern Italy, known to the Greeks as "Magna Graecia."
The temple in Paestum (the Greek Posidonia) and the sanctuary of Poseidon,
or Hera II, built in the middle of the fifth century BC, are perfect examples of classical Doric architecture.

The El Djem amphitheater (previously Thysdrus), the largest in Africa,
was begun during the reign of Emperor Septimus Severus, but remained unfinished because of unrest in 238 AD
during Gordian II's ascension to the Roman throne.

Detail of an Ephesian bas-relief representing the helmet and leg armor of Greco-Roman armament from Asia. ▷

THE IMPACT OF ROME

According to the legend, Romulus founded Rome on the shores of the Tiber in 753 BC.
During the first five hundred years the town had to confront an impressive number of enemies: Albins, Etruscans,
Oscs, Ombrians, Veians, to cite only a few of the restless neighbors hoping to destroy the young city.
Then the Gaulois swept down upon Latium, twice destroying the incipient Roman economy.
Subjected by Sabine and then Etruscan kings, Rome overthrew the monarchical regime to become a republic
with an unabashed imperialistic appetite.

THE CONQUEST OF THE WESTERN MEDITERRANEAN

In fact, things happened very quickly. In a single century, Roman legions subjected the Samnites, annexed Etruria and seized what was called "Magna Graecia," that is, southern Italy and Sicily. Moreover, it was in Sicily that for the first time the Romans encountered Greek civilization, which was so deeply to influence their culture. But, contemporaneously, in 265 BC, the Romans also confronted the soldiers of another great power that had ruled the western Mediterranean for nearly one hundred years, the Carthaginians, distant descendants of Phoenician sailors who had founded several outposts in Sicily. The conflict quickly spread beyond Sicily and became what was subsequently called the First Punic War, for the word *poeni*, as the Romans called the Carthaginians. Because they were considerably weaker than their enemies at sea, the Romans chose to transfer the conflict onto the land. After several reversals, they finally carried the day. Sicily became their first province and Carthage was obliged to pay a heavy yearly tribute. The opulent North African city, however, was able to gather its forces due, above all, to the energy of Hamilcar Barca, the powerful and popular head of the Barcid clan. Realizing that the defeat of Carthage had resulted from its economic weakness and its congenital lack of interest in non-coastal areas,

Hamilcar Barca and his son Hannibal invaded Spain in order to seize the rich copper, iron and tin mines and to establish trading posts along the Iberian coast. In a few years, they had built a veritable empire. In 218 BC, Hannibal laid siege to the Spanish cities allied to Rome, the most important of which was Saguntum. This attack was the prelude to the Second Punic War, which lasted less than seven months. Never since its founding had Rome been so close to defeat. Hannibal's troops, after crossing the Alps, took the Roman legions from behind and gained victory after victory. The Carthaginians were outnumbered by three to one, yet fought valiantly against the 240,000 strong Roman army. Scipio Africanus, a Roman general, succeeded in fomenting a general revolt against Carthage by rallying the main Spanish and North African leaders to his cause. Discouraged, Hannibal returned to defend his country. Scipio followed his enemy and defeated him at the battle of Zama in 202 BC.

Thus did the brilliant African city of Carthage meet its end. Heavily taxed by war tributes, it tried in vain to shake off the Roman yoke by launching the Third Punic War of in 149 BC. The Roman retaliated mercilessly and Carthage was definitively wiped off the map. Now the entire western half of the Mediterranean was under Roman influence.

A partial view of Pompeii, the largest of the three cities buried in 79AD by Etna's unexpected eruption. The other two cities were Herculanum and Stabies.

With Etna in the background, the Taormina theater is a magnificent example of the Hellenistic-Latin architectural genius. It was begun in the third century BC by the Greeks under Geron II, then rebuilt and completed by the Romans four centuries later.

The sanctuary of Tanith, the goddess of fertility, in Salammbo, near Carthage.
Many funeral steles with signs of the Punic deity can be found, especially in the area devoted to child sacrifices.

The city of Dugga (the ancient city of Thugga) in Tunisia is one of the best preserved Roman sites in Africa.
It was built during the second and third centuries on a former Phoenician construction.

The conquest of the eastern Mediterranean

Until that time in history, the Romans had had to wage a series of defensive wars, first against the Gaulois, then their Italian neighbors and finally the Carthaginians. At the start of the second century Roman mentality was beginning to change. For the first time both its leaders and its people desired to conquer new lands, and extend the territory of the mother country. They naturally looked eastward towards a region the Romans knew, having fought Philip V's Macedonian troops aiding the Carthaginians. This was the beginning of Roman imperialism. Roman armies began by attacking Macedonia, officially to "free" the Greeks. Then they turned against the Galates, a people of Asia Minor who were struggling against the king of Pergame, a Roman ally. During the third Macedonian War, Roman soldiers permanently dismembered the kingdoms of Macedonia and Illyria. Then, in the name of Pax Romana, they simply annexed all of Greece, which had been impudent enough to rise up against Roman abuses in Macedonia.

Roman advances in the east slowed when trouble in Spain began to threaten the Roman republic. The Roman Senate decided that priority must be given to restoring order in the western provinces. Despite the valiant resistance of the Celtibers and Lusitanians, massive intervention by Roman legions brought an overwhelming victory and "peace" to the Iberian Peninsula. Rome then proceeded to counter the rebellious tribes of southern Gaul. After these revolts were subdued, the Roman Republic had to contend with a series of civil wars and uprisings in Italy that shook it to its foundations. Providential leaders such as Sylla, Pompey and, of course, Caesar appeared who were able to settle domestic conflicts and maintain fear of the central power abroad. After meeting the challenge in the west, Rome again returned to its conquest of the east. Its principal enemy at the end of the second century BC was the powerful king of Pontus, Mithridate, whose imperialistic expansion opposed the Romans in the northeastern Mediterranean and threatened

their trade. After three wars, Rome finally was able to defeat Mithridate. Without breaking their stride, Roman armies went on to seize all of Macedonia and Asia Minor which they divided into four provinces, Asia, Bithhynia, Cilicie and Pontus. This was followed by the signing of alliances with the kingdoms of Cappadocia and Galatia, relegating them to the status of Roman colonies. At this same time Caesar completed his conquest of the Gauls and proceeded to annex Egypt.

Pompeii's remarkable state of preservation is due to the fact that it was protected from the vicissitudes of the weather by the pumice and lava under which it was buried.

*Exceptional evidence of the refinement and wealth of first century Roman life
was unearthed by the archeological excavations.*

Unlike Pompeii, Herculaneum was literally "petrified" by the volcanic mudflow.
The inhabitants did not have time to flee. Here more than elsewhere the visitor has the impression of "suspended life."

Distant view and detail of Celsus's library,
built around 120 AD and characteristic of what is known as "imperial art,"
a blending of oriental architectural styles and monumental Roman scale.
Before it and to the right of the paved roadway is Hadrian's small temple.

POLICEMEN OF THE MEDITERRANEAN

Egypt attempted a final revolt when Mark Anthony, Cleopatra's lover, at the head of 120,000 soldiers in 500 warships attacked the Roman fleet led by Agrippa and Caesar's nephew, Octavian, off the coast of Actium in 31 BC. Mark Anthony was beaten and his fall brought down the Ptolemaic dynasty of Egypt. Rome was now absolute master of the entire Mediterranean. Octavian continued his conquest of the Middle East. Thanks to the great popular favor his victories had brought, he had himself appointed Emperor in 27 BC, ascending the Roman throne as Augustus Caesar and ending three hundred years of republican government. The Golden Age of Rome began with Augustus Caesar. At the height of its military power, the Italian capital imposed its law everywhere, acting as a policeman throughout the known world. With its far-flung administration, well trained and equipped legions and, above all, the unconditionally enthusiastic and overwhelming support of its people, Rome "ruled the universe," for over two centuries.

A friend of Augustus, the famous Mecen, began the tradition of wealthy patrons of art and literature. Some of mankind's most majestic monuments were erected contemporaneously with the works of Virgil, Ovid, Horace and Seneca. The

The Arimondi fountain in Rethimnon is an interesting example of Roman architecture as adapted to eastern and Cretan tastes.

Both a tenth-century Arab bridge
and a well preserved Roman bridge
span the Guadalevín River in Ronda, Spain.

glory of Rome endured during the reigns of twelve Caesars, the Flavians and the Antonins. However, in the year 138 AD, when Trajan, the last of the Antonins died, the Roman Empire began to crack, a victim of its own excessiveness. There were three main causes of its rapid fall. The first was without doubt its size: the Senate was unable to run an area covering seven million square kilometers. The second was the advent and the success of monotheistic Christianity, which rapidly revealed itself quite sectarian. Once the Emperor Constantine had been won over to its cause, the new religion was quick to forbid all other faiths. Common people were now deprived of their beneficent gods and no longer able to recognize themselves in leaders who betrayed their ancestral values. Finally, there was the increasing rebelliousness of vanquished peoples who finally dared to oppose the central power.

The mortal blow to the failing empire was delivered by the Emperor Theodusius, a versatile, quick-tempered Spaniard who imposed Christianism on the peoples of the Roman empire, all of whom - Greeks, Egyptians, Africans, Arabs and Persians - had religions of their own and rejected the new faith. In 395 AD Theodusius divided the empire in two, giving the east to his son Arcadius and the west to his other son, Honorius. A homogeneous Roman Empire ceased to exist and rivalry between the eastern and western parts of the former empire increased as the years went by. Cut off from eastern resources, the Western Empire quickly succumbed to the conjugated assaults of the Barbarians. In the year 401, Alaric, the Visigoth king, sacked Rome. Vandals, Burgonds, Ostrogoths, Alains, and Huns shared among themselves the carcass of their former master. The Eastern Empire was relatively unaffected by these events and survived for nearly one thousand years as the Byzantine Empire.

Built in the first century as part of a 50-kilometer long aqueduct to bring 30,000 to 40,000 liters of fresh water daily to Nimes, the 273-meter-long Pont du Gard aqueduct has three rows of arches reaching 49 meters in height.

The Varrlaam monastery is one of the most typical of the famous "aerial" monasteries Orthodox monks began building on rock pinnacles, Meteora, in Thessaly during the fourteenth century in order to find meditative peace.

Orthodox paintings are the direct heirs to Byzantine art as influenced by Russian taste. ▷

BYZANTINES, ARABS AND CRUSADERS

In the year 330, Emperor Constantine founded on both shores of the Bosporus a city to which he gave his name, Constantinople. Upon the fall of the Western Roman Empire, all the traditional classical Roman values took refuge in this city of renown. It commanded the wealthy provinces of Syria, Palestine and Egypt and welcomed to its court the intelligentsia of Antioch and Alexandria. It was also served by an efficient administration and a reliable, faithful and remarkably well equipped army. Still, relations between the emperors and the heavily taxed war-weary people were troubled. Sensing that the time was ripe for newcomers, the Arabs, took advantage of these failings and swept in.

JUSTINIAN AND THE ADVENT OF THE BYZANTINE EMPIRE

In 527, Emperor Justinian, a scholar and astute politician, ascended the eastern throne. This pragmatic Christian was skilled at reducing the ethnic and religious conflicts that threatened the Byzantine state, with the aid of Empress Theodora, an exceptional woman who gave new luster to the tarnished image of the sovereigns. After reinforcing the basis of his power and improving the domestic economy, Justinian turned to foreign policy. He signed an "eternal peace" treaty with Persia, accepting to pay a colossal amount of gold in exchange for guaranteed peace on his eastern borders. Then he undertook to reconquer those territories that formerly belonged to the Western Roman Empire. General Belisar invaded North Africa without meeting any resistance, crossed the Mediterranean and seized one after the other Naples and Rome, thus driving the Visigoths further north.

In fewer than ten years, Byzantine troops had taken all of Italy and southern Spain from the Barbarians, turning them back from the shores of the Mediterranean, which once again became a Roman sea. After restoring peace, Justinian proceeded to the final stage of his project: establishing a code of justice. Despite its imperfections, the document made the Byzantine Empire the first "modern" state in the world.

In spite of appearances, the state remained fragile. The central Barbarians, particularly the Bulgars, had sacked Greece more than once and had even laid unsuccessful siege to Constantinople. Internal religious rivalries among Orthodox Christians, Monophysites and Nestorians were at work, weakening the central authority. In the west, the Franks, descendants of older Barbarian peoples, appeared, first invading Gaul in 500 and then Aquitaine. They founded a powerful kingdom that stretched from the Pyrenees to the Rhine. The Byzantine emperors were concerned by the emergence of these western powers that were slowly dispossessing them of their territory. Yet, whether from lack of will power or lack of resources, they did not intervene. Vast territories were thus left unoccupied, an open invitation to peoples bent on expansion.

General view of Mistra, the hill overlooking the plain of Sparta
in the Peloponnese. On the hillside are the most outstanding examples
of sacred Greek Orthodox art of the fourteenth and fifteenth centuries.
The Perivletos monastery (here, the main entrance)
is renowned for its paintings and frescos.

Another example of the blending of Arab, Byzantine and Norman styles is the Palatine Chapel built by Roger II
in the center of the Norman Palace. It was completed in 1140 and dedicated to Saint Peter.
The walls and ceiling are covered with magnificent mosaics and there is a huge Christ Pantocrator in the apse.

Saint-Jean of the Hermits church, erected by Roger II in 1132,
is the most typical monument of the Byzantine-Norman style in Sicily.
Red oriental style cupolas top the sober gray construction characteristic of medieval European architecture.

Il Duomo or the dome in Montreale is an example of the blending of medieval Byzantine, Arab and Norman influences. Founded in 1174 by William II, this imposing Sicilian basilica was designed on a Latin plan with three naves and a Byzantine sanctuary without a cupola.

View of the large interior courtyard of the cloister in the Benedictine convent,
adjoining the main Romanesque church built at the same time.

With its huge central cupola 31 meters in diameter rising to a height of 55 meters above the ground, Saint Sophia is considered the masterpiece of Byzantine architecture. It was constructed from 532 to 537 AD on orders from Emperor Justinian and subsequently became a mosque after the Turkish capture of Constantinople in 1453.

Constantinople protected the entrance to the Bosporus by a line of outposts and forts that Mehmed II seized in 1452
as he began the siege of the Byzantine capital. In their stead he built the Rumeli Hisari fortress to keep the Christian flotillas
from coming to the city's aid.

*Part view of the interior courtyard of the Great Mosque of the Ommiades in Damascus, built in 705 by al-Walid,
the sixth caliph. The octagonal building in the foreground is the Treasury Cupola, which used to store public funds.*

*Muslim art was transformed by local taste. Bab al Khamis is one of the gates to the imperial city of Meknes,
Morocco, where Maulay Isma'il ruled from 1672 to 1727.*

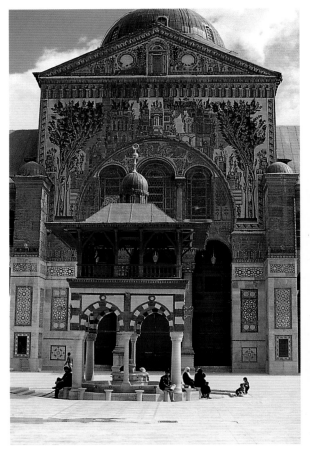

THE WILD RIDE OF THE ARABS

While the Byzantines were looking to the west, another flag was being raised in the east, in the wide-open spaces of Arabia. The standard was green and bore the arms of the Prophet. Like a desert wind, it announced a terrible storm that was to carry away everything it encountered along its path. Its spiritual and military guide was Mohammed, a member of the powerful Kouraïchite family, who had been masters of Mecca since the sixth century. In 611 Mohammed received a divine revelation and became the Prophet of the Arab nation. Eleven years later, he and his companions captured the city of Medina and initiated the *hegira*, or the beginning of the Muslim era. There he preached the *jihad* or holy war against Islam's enemies. In 630 AD, after defeating his opponents, he entered Mecca which then became his capital. When Mohammed died two years later, his successors began a veritable triumphant march. By the strength of their arms as well as the inspiration of their fanatic faith, Muslim troops carved out an immense empire with a rapidity that has always astonished historians. One can judge for oneself: in 633 Iraq was seized from the Sassanids of Persia, between 635 and 638 Syria was taken from the Byzantines, in 638-640 the Iranian territories of Khouzistan and Choustar fell before Iran was totally annexed in 642. In 639 Egypt was conquered; in 643 it was Libya's turn. Only internal struggles between supporters and adversaries of Ali, the Prophet's nephew, momentarily slowed the conquerors' advance. These brief, yet violent,

*The high walls topped by thirty-six towers of the impressive Anamur fort dominate the waters of the Mediterranean.
The Emirs of Karakorum built it in 1230 on the site of an early Roman fort
that had been transformed into a castle by Armenian rulers.*

▷

The Great Mosque of Sidi Uqba ibn Nafi, in Kairouan, Tunisia, was erected first in 670 AD, then rebuilt in 703, 772 and 836. The current buildings, most of wich date from the eighth and ninth centuries are among the masterpieces of Islam. ▷

Persian style interior porticos in the Al-Azhar Mosque in Cairo, founded by the Fatimids in the tenth century. It houses the second largest Koranic university in the Arab world.

encounters gave rise to the two main branches of Islam, Sunnism and Shi'ism. The winners of this struggle, the Ommaid caliphs, then resumed the conquests. In 670 their horsemen invaded southern Tunisia, then in 698 the Aures Mountains in Algeria. By 710 they controlled all of the Maghrib which converted to Islam. Only a few indomitable bastions continued to resist for a short period in Kabylie in Algeria and in the Moroccan Atlas and Rif Mountains. Converted Berber leaders carried on the Arab conquerors' role and invaded southern Spain, vanquishing it in 713. They created splendid powerful kingdoms. In their heyday, these Moorish soldiers made raids as far north as Poitiers in western France. On several occasions they tried to invade the Frankish Merovingian kingdom.

Meanwhile, far to the east, other Muslim troops conquered the Sind and settled in Samarkand in Uzbekistan. In the middle of the seventh century, the Abassids ousted the Ommiads of Damascus and founded what was to be their capital, the city of Baghdad. Only when their armies crushed the Chinese in Talas in 750-751 was the Muslim conquest totally complete. Thus, in less than one century, the surprising Muslim military power, born of alliances among former enemy Bedouin tribes, had carved out a colossal empire stretching from Turkestan to Spain. It had defeated states thousands of years old and had eliminated some others, such as the Sassanid Persians. The Arabs, however, were not mere warriors; they made a substantial contribution to Mediterranean culture. Soon, incomparably fine handicrafts, damask and silk fabrics, paper - techniques whose secrets they had learned from the Chinese - rugs, perfumes and glass appeared on occidental markets strongly influencing traditional western artisans' techniques. The arts and sciences flourished to such an extent that historians do not hesitate to speak of an "Arab miracle" as they did of the "Greek miracle" centuries earlier. For three hundred years, from 750 to 1100, all the scholars of the Mediterranean world were Arab or under their influence. After serving first as a "bridge" between the accomplishments of Greek and Chinese sciences, the Arabs themselves made an enormous number of inventions in the fields of astronomy, mathematics, physics, medicine, botany, geography, philosophy and history. Mediterranean trade flourished. Caravans transported oriental products to the great Levantine ports from which merchant fleets dispatched them to cities in the central and western Mediterranean area. The Arabs also

introduced new fashions in the lifestyles of these countries: orchards, ingenious systems of irrigation, terraced farming, and large interior gardens, with shade trees and fountains, in palaces and great homes. We owe to them the many fruits, citrus and vegetables that stock our market stalls and that were unknown in the region before the Arab invasion.

While other nations crumbled before the tumultuous wave of the Arab conquest, the Byzantine Empire alone resisted its attacks. The eastern empire had even inflicted crushing defeats on the Muslims in 677 and 717 before the walls of Constantinople and in Akroinon in Asia Minor in 740, but had lost some of its richest provinces, including Egypt, Syria and Palestine with its holy places, as well as the Mediterranean coast of Africa. Moreover, on its western flank, the Byzantine Empire had a new enemy, Charlemagne, crowned emperor

of the Franks in 800. He detested Constantinople whose orthodox religion he considered a heresy. This led him to sign secret agreements with the caliph Haroun al Rachid in order to organize a pincer strategy to surround the eastern Christian Empire. In 802 and 806 Arab troops encountered Byzantine armies heading towards Syria. The Arabs defeated them, since the Byzantine Empire had been seriously weakened by both internal rivalries and conflicts with the Carolingians and was on the verge of collapse. At the end of the ninth century, however, a new Macedonian dynasty mounted the throne in Constantinople. Its rulers succeeded in improving the economy, which had suffered from so many years of war. They also took advantage of the weakness of the Carolingian Empire. Starting in the year 1000 Emperor Basil II reconquered Syria, advanced to the Armenian border and

Abd el Rahman I had the mosque in Cordoba built from 785 to 788. Its plan copies that of the Al-Aqsa Mosque in Jerusalem. After being enlarged on several occasions by Muslim princes it was transformed into a cathedral in the thirteenth century.

Detail of one of the remarkable sculpted ceilings of the Great Mosque of Cordoba.

ruthlessly crushed the Bulgars. The second golden Age of Byzantine, its most brilliant and stable period, was about to begin. Two events took place, however, that were indicative of the Empire's basic fragility.

Despite valiant efforts, the Byzantine fleet was unable to prevent conquering Normans, sailors from colder northern climes, from settling in Sicily after its partial occupation by the Arabs in the ninth century. Secondly, it was unable to put down a revolt by mercenaries who, having defied its power, left the Byzantine sphere of influence with impunity. Indeed, the Byzantine army consisted of large contingents of foreigners that it could no longer afford to pay. One after the other, powerless emperors saw their difficulties increase. After taking Armenia, the Turks pressed hard upon the northern Byzantine border.

The long-term difference with Rome led to the great Christian schism, which in the eleventh century permanently separated Roman Catholics from Orthodox Christians. 1071 was a terrible year for the Byzantines. They lost the battle of Mantzikert, relinquishing Central Asia to the Turks, and were driven out of Italy by the Normans. The superb city of Constantinople was beginning its slow demise.

In the sixteenth century, the Knights of Saint John erected the Kamyros Castle on the western coast of Rhodes.

The Maltese Islands contain innumerable monuments constructed by the Knights of Malta. The Victoria citadel,
built in the fifteenth century, offers a view of the Island of Gozo and allowed the inhabitants to resist pirates and the Turks.

*The immense castle in Aigues Mortes, Provence, is now landlocked,
but was a major Mediterranean port in the Middle Ages.*

THE TIMES OF THE CRUSADES

In 1095 at the Council of Clermont, Pope Urban II preached in favor of the First Crusade to free Christ's tomb and the holy places in Palestine from the Muslims. Two years later Jerusalem fell to Christian horsemen. The First Crusade ended with the creation of the Frankish kingdom of Syria and Palestine, the crusader states. This part of the Middle East had always been inhabited by Muslims, Jews and Orthodox Christians who were thereafter subject to the harsh feudal model imported from the west.

There were seven other Crusades between 1147 and 1270. All were characterized by violence and pillaging. The resentment felt by the vanquished led to numerous revolts and was the start of the great disharmony between the Muslim and Christian worlds that still exists today. The Byzantine emperors could not understand why a wave of Christian fanaticism was unfurling. They refused to admit that Christian priests could carry the cross and be stained with human blood. This growing lack of understanding between western and eastern Christians would eventually be settled to the detriment

of the latter. The two French lords who led the Fourth Crusade simply diverted it from the Holy Land in order to attack Constantinople! The Venetians played a sinister role. Their merchants had been present in Constantinople for several centuries, but were expelled in 1171 because of their excessive financial demands and most important, their propensity to foment trouble in state affairs. Hoping both to reestablish their profitable trade and to take vengeance for the insult, they financed the Fourth Crusade and maneuvered brilliantly so that the crusaders took the city of Zara and then Constantinople in "payment of their debt" to the Venetians. The prestigious Byzantine city was seized after two assaults and then sacked. Despite an ultimate attempt by the Byzantine armies dispatched from Asia Minor to defend their country, the Empire was dismantled. The Crusaders divided the spoils amongst them, setting up the Latin Empire in Constantinople and the Kingdom of Thessaloniki, while Venice appropriated most of the maritime possessions, including Crete, Euboea and all the Aegean and Ionian Islands, thus strengthening its

own trade monopoly in the Mediterranean. This unhealed wound festered, poisoning the souls of oriental Christians who often remained neutral in wars between Crusaders and Muslims, sometimes going so far as to aid the latter. The only consolation the Byzantine survivors found was Nicaea where they took refuge and founded a small empire of the same name. The Genovese, the secular rivals of the Venetians, became their allies. The Nicaean Empire spread southward gaining control of the Peloponnese and holding it until the middle of the fifteenth century. The Muslims, on the other hand, had absorbed the impact of the Crusades and reorganized their

forces. The Turks carried on for the Arabs who had borne the brunt of the Crusaders' first frontal attacks. Charismatic leaders, such as Nureddin and his son Saladin, led the Islamic troops in victory, seizing Syria and Palestine from the Franks. At the beginning of the fourteenth century the last Crusaders were forced out of the Levant by the repeated attacks of the Mamluks, who had recently arrived from Egypt under the command of Sultan Baybars. The Mediterranean fell under the control of the Muslim fleet and the Saracens, as westerners called followers of the Prophet, dominated the entire Mediterranean area for several centuries.

Kolossi Castle, Cyprus, built in the thirteenth century, was reconstructed as we know it in the middle of the fifteenth century.
During the fourteenth century it was the seat of the Great Commandery of the Knights of the Order of Saint John of Jerusalem,
and in the sixteenth, of the Knight Templars.

Kiz Kalesi Castle or "castle of the young woman," located on the southern coast of eastern Turkey, was erected in the twelfth century by the Armenian rulers who governed Cilicia until 1375. A long dike of which some vestiges remain connected it to the shore.

Near the port of Kato Paphos, Cyprus, rise the ruins of the Frankish Santa Kolones Castle, erected by the Lusignan family at the end of the twelfth century on the site of an earlier Byzantine fort.

The large interior courtyard of Saint Gilles Castle on the Al Rifayyat hill in Tripoli, Lebanon, one of the most famous Crusader fortresses in the Holy Land. Raymond of Saint Gilles had it built in the twelfth century.

The low silhouette of the twelfth-century Crusader fortress known as the "Castle of the Sea." It was built of the site of an old Phoenician temple on a small island in the Bay of Sayda (Sidon) and linked by a dike to the mainland.

Interior view of the Crusader Castle in Byblos (present day Jybayl in Lebanon)
which during the Crusades was part of the County of Tripoli.

Monolithos Castle, built by the Order of the Knights of Rhodes at the summit of an impressive rocky peak,
overlooks the superb bay that opens onto the Karpathos Sea.

The church of San Giorgio Maggiore in the Venetian lagoon was built from an old Benedictine convent on the island.
It was altered and enlarged several times, most notably under the direction of Andrea Palladio in the sixteenth century.
The more recent additions date from the seventeenth century.

The Venetian lion, common throughout the Mediterranean, attests to the exceptional influence of the City of the Doges. ▷

ITALIAN IMPRINT FROM THE XIIITH TO THE XVITH CENTURY

Mediterranean trade was in the hands of the Saracens who controlled most of the commercial relations between the Orient and the advanced western bastions of Sicily, Sardinia, Corsica and the Balearic Islands. To the west, fast Barbary vessels based in North Africa constantly threatened the few European ships that ventured onto the seas. Western economy had been strangled by weak trade exchanges and rudimentary handicrafts and was in a pitiful state of stagnation. At the beginning of the 13th century, however, the situation changed under the impetus of brilliant Italian financiers capable of allying a fine sense of diplomacy and a surprising "capitalist" view of the economy. They introduced the judicious use of farm surpluses and developed large business-oriented cities.

THE VENETIAN REPUBLIC

Lombards from the large northern Italian cities dominated the Middle Ages. These rich merchants and wealthy bankers introduced new revolutionary business practices and financial techniques, such as accounting, investments, investment management, bank loans and letters of exchange. Tuscan innovators took over from the early Lombards. These men became indispensable to European kings and emperors who turned to them for credit to finance their wars and Crusades. By the end of the 11th century, the Italian financiers' covert political power was considerable.

By the time the Crusades ended, two centuries later, these men had made themselves the indispensable partners to heads of state and played important parts in all political and economic transactions. As owners of the fleets that carried Crusaders to the Holy Land, they had firmly established their influence. They had developed commercial bases in the eastern territories of Constantinople, Alexandria, Jerusalem and Adana long before anyone else. As the Byzantine Empire entered its final throes after the fall of Constantinople in 1204, four Italian cities, Genoa, Florence, Pisa and especially Venice, had divided the Mediterranean trade monopoly among themselves. The 13th century found them at the apex of their power. Venice, better known as the city of the Doges or the Serenissima, "most serene city," possessed three major advantages. On the domestic front, it had such a powerful system of banks that it was automatically the intermediary for any European sovereign wishing to embark on military or scientific expeditions. It controlled the western points of departure of the silk, spice and fur routes. Finally, it possessed rapid warships and a powerful merchant fleet that even the Saracens dreaded. Flaunting the pompous title of "Lords of the Sea," the Venetians, in fact, ruled over a vast maritime empire that included both shores of the Adriatic, a good part of Greece, the Aegean Islands, Crete and over half of the former Byzantine Empire. The Serene Republic's financial strategists had devised a clever system called the *colleganza* which allied a banker or a financier in Venice with a merchant who assumed the hazards of the voyage and the commercial risks abroad. Profits of such ventures were shared equally on the merchant's return. There were dozens of Venetian commercial bases along the Mediterranean coastline.

The Venetians mastered the consummate art of alliance making, and whenever it served their commercial interests, employed sly covert diplomacy to "bind" their friends as well as their enemies. The Italian city had signed trade agreements

with the Muslims to protect its ships from Arab and Barbary attacks, while at the same time signing other treaties with the Mongols who had just vanquished the Muslims in Central Asia. Playing one off against the other in both the east and the west, Venice became the dominant Mediterranean power, without its armies ever conquering any territory. Its influence extended from one end of the Mediterranean to the other.

The Isle of Bourzi in the Bay of Nauplie, Greece, holds a charming little Venetian fort.
Two imposing citadels dominate the city itself and testify to the long Venetian occupation.

Alfonso of Aragon erected the Renaissance gate between two towers of Castelnuovo in Naples.
Work began in 1453 and was unfinished at the time of the monarch's death.
The Lombard architect Pietro da Milan completed it in 1466.

Two columns topped by does at the entrance to the port of Madraki are believed to indicate the location
of the feet of the huge colossus that, according to tradition, spanned the waters here.
The monumental statue indeed existed, but was not erected here.

Like certain other buildings located on the other side of the port, Fort Koules is one of the last vestiges of the Venetian
occupation of Crete between the thirteenth and seventeenth centuries.

Despite its reconstruction by the Turks, the old city of Iraklion has preserved some of its famous seventeenth-century "oriental Venetian fountains," such as the Bempo fountain and the Morosini fountain whose lions support a fourteenth-century basin.

Construction of the Cathedral of Santa Maria del Fiore, Florence, began in 1294, but was interrupted at the death of its architect Arnolfo di Cambio in 1302. Work began again in 1332 with the building of the Campanile by Giotto. After 16 years of labor, the entire cathedral was completed in 1436. Brunelleschi's famous dome was constructed without the traditional armature and has become a symbol of the Italian Renaissance.

GENOA, PISA, FLORENCE AND THE CONDOTTIERI

Genovese, Pisans and Florentines came to Constantinople during the 12th century, nearly two hundred years after their rivals, the Venetians. The struggle for predominance was bitter, if unavowed. Despite their use of assertive, far-reaching statesmanship, the newcomers were unable to supplant the Venetians until the fall of the Byzantine Empire. Each city endeavored to carve out a private sphere of influence where its supremacy was unchallenged. Thus, the Pisans attempted to open permanent settlements in western Mediterranean, but were beaten first by the Genovese fleet in 1284, before they succumbed to Florentine domination at the beginning of

the 15th century. The Florentines, on the other hand, were more interested in the northern Mediterranean coast, where they met with varying degrees of success. Their influence on maritime affairs was weak, because the Florentine economy was land oriented. The Genovese proved to be worthy rivals of the Venetians on the seas, and were their mortal enemies. Throughout the 13th century, despite the hostility of the Venetians and Pisans, Genoa was able to hold a powerful maritime empire in the eastern Mediterranean. Many traces of the Genovese remain in the Ionian and Aegean Islands, Crete, Cyprus and along the western coast of Asia Minor. At

The Tuscan city of San Gimignano is known as the "city of beautiful towers," because of the fortress-homes constructed by wealthy families in the thirteenth century. Only thirteen of the seventy-six tower-residences remain, testifying to the wealth and power of their owners who vied for prestige by erecting taller and taller buildings.

With its alternating bands of white and black stones, Santa Trinita Saccargia, near the Sardinian village of Codrongianos is a typical example of Pisan architecture of the twelfth and thirteenth centuries.

The principal monument in Oristano, Sardinia, illustrates the blending
of thirteenth-century Gothic with fourteenth-century Pisan and Spanish styles.
The island was under Arab then Spanish domination for two centuries.

the height of their rivalry, Venice and Genoa hired the services of the famous *condottieri*, mercenaries who fought with their own private business-like armies. The conflicts and provocations increased in Italy and abroad, in the Mediterranean commercial bases. This intense competition resulted in the first major confrontation in the Gulf of Laias in 1294 during which the Genovese Admiral Spinola crushed the Venetian fleet. The Venetians decided to revenge the insult by attacking their adversary's merchant fleet everywhere in the Mediterranean. The Genovese responded in kind. Convoys could not expect to arrive safely at their destinations. The Barbary pirates took advantage of this situation to renew their own attacks. The situation worsened, degenerating into open warfare. By laying waste to the main Genovese commercial bases, the Venetian admirals Malabranca and Soranza endangered Genoa's large slave and aluminum markets in central and eastern Mediterranean. At last, Genoa sent its leading sailor, Admiral Doria, to attack the Venetian fleet in the Otranto Canal, inflicting on the City of the Doges the most crushing defeat in its history. Eighty out of the ninety-

six Venetian galleys were destroyed or captured. Seven thousand Venetians were killed and eighty thousand were taken prisoner. The famous Marco Polo was one of the latter. Indeed, He wrote *Discovery of the World* during his imprisonment in Genoa.

In the face of defeat, Venice had no choice but to sign a peace treaty with its rival. The Genovese were now in control of most of the eastern Mediterranean. A brief period of peace ensued during which the two adversaries renewed their strength and sought new allies, while collaborating to curb the Barbary States. The Venetians, however, could not forgive and forget. In the 15th century, they took advantage of the aggressiveness of the Turks, recent newcomers to the Mediterranean, to attack the Genovese. They succeeded in destroying the naval supremacy of Genoa and forced it to abandon all of its commercial bases in the Mediterranean. After contributing to the fall of the Byzantine Empire, it defeated and ruined its Italian rivals, and in contempt of all morality, opened the way for the Turks whose insatiable appetite would devour the Venetians as well as the entire Mediterranean basin.

Piazza del Campo in Sienna.
Elegant thirteenth-century palaces line
the shell-shaped place where every year
since 1283 the famous palio (costumed
festival) has taken place.

The entrance to the Gulf of Porto is
dominated by Genovese towers.
All those on the island were built
during their occupation from the twelfth
to the fourteenth centuries.

In the distance, opposite the large
Genovese tower that dominates Santa
Teresa di Gallura in Sardinia appear
the coastlines of the Lavezzi Islands
and Corsica.

The remarkable fluted Yivli Minare was added to a former church by Aladdin Kaïkobad at the beginning of the thirteenth century. It is one of the most interesting monuments in Antalya.

In Bursa, a detail of the turbe (mausoleum) of Prince Mehmed, son of Bayezid I, a fourteenth-century Ottoman sovereign. ▷

FROM THE OTTOMAN EMPIRE TO MODERN TIMES

The fifteenth century was a time of radical changes in the Mediterranean and great upheavals throughout Europe. Christendom had been beset by internal fighting for one hundred years. To escape from Italian intrigues the papacy took refuge in Avignon, then returned to Rome in 1376. Internecine rivalries in the Vatican were such that there were soon two popes and then three, after the Council of Pisa in 1409. Matters returned to normal with the humanist Popes of mid-century, but wounds were long in healing. The fifteenth century also marked the beginning of the first important round-the-world sailing expeditions and great discoveries. In 1492, Christopher Columbus touched land on the American continent. In the Mediterranean, Venetian military and trade supremacy ceded to the Ottoman Turks and by the beginning of the 15th century the Mediterranean belonged to the sultan of Istanbul.

GRANDEUR AND DECADENCE OF THE OTTOMAN EMPIRE

The Turks were the uncontested masters of Central Asia, more so even than the Mongols. At the beginning of the 13th century, Uthman or Osman, a prince of the Oghouzs, a Turkmen tribe living in Anatolia, had greatly enlarged the kingdom inherited from his father and he became the first sovereign of a new dynasty that bore his name. Overconfident of his strength, he had tried unsuccessfully to vanquish the Byzantine Empire. His successors, particularly his son, Orhan, the veritable founder of the Ottoman Empire, relentlessly pursued this undertaking. In one century, they had constructed an economic and military power that rivaled the principal medieval states. Then they set out to conquer. The first to succumb was the Byzantine Empire. Constantinople was taken in eight short weeks of siege in 1453. Next to fall were Greece, Egypt, Syria, Persia, Hungary and Iraq. Under Süleyman the Magnificent, the Ottoman Empire extended from Budapest to Aden and from Tabriz to Annaba. There were more and more incursions along the Italian and Spanish coasts. Western countries were incapable of standing up to the might of these violent Muslims. A few cities, among them Venice, signed treaties of non-aggression with the Turks and for a short time preserved their trade acquisitions. The sultan reigned over both the Orient and the West. The Mediterranean had become an Ottoman lake. The Ottomans owed their supremacy to both their arms and their administration. Their artillery was modern with large cannons that could fire 1,200-pound cannonballs that effectively silenced their enemies' medieval guns. Their highly centralized imperial administration mastered the art of delegating responsibility at every level, enabling it to provide stores to the army and to govern the recently conquered provinces almost immediately after the fighting. The imperial territory was divided into districts, which were subdivided into fiefs. The head of this pyramid was located in Topkapi, the sultan's palace, where twenty thousand people worked. Istanbul, with over 600,000 inhabitants, was the largest European city of its time. For over three centuries Ottoman hegemony over the Mediterranean was uncontested. Yet various conflicts with other states proved that they were not invincible. Their fleet had been soundly beaten at Lepanto in 1571 by the troops of Don John of Austria. The impression of calm superiority that emanated from the empire discouraged their adversaries from even contemplating combat. This was reinforced by the fact that many European countries had signed trade agreements and non-aggression treaties with the Turks. In addition, the West was busy with its own concerns. Catholics and Protestants

The "Blue Mosque" or the Mosque of Sultan Mehmed in Istanbul was built between 1609 and 1616 by the architect Mehmed Aga. Its name is derived form the many blue and green mosaics that decorate its walls. It houses a madrasa (Koranic school) and a imaret (Muslim hospice). It is the only mosque with six minarets.

were fighting bloody religious wars, bringing chaos to entire nations. Peasant revolts followed insurrections by the nobility. Spain and Portugal were fighting for possession of the New World. The European kings' unbridled pursuit of conquest brought disaster to national economies and dilapidated the inheritance of past centuries. Like all great empires throughout history, the Ottoman state would eventually discover the perverse effects of its own excessiveness. The sultan, "Commander of the Faithful", ruled the eastern Mediterranean as absolute master, sowing terror from Gibraltar to the Persian Gulf. The tasks of maintaining order and putting down rebellions were enormous, even for the most powerful fleet of the era. Moreover, more than half of the inhabitants of the empire lived in poverty under the weight of a feudal-like administration. Corruption and incompetence gnawed away at the state administration. The Janissary corps, the imperial crack troops, often revolted, killing more than one sultan. In order to survive, the Ottomans had to relax their hold. They established friendlier relations with some of the more influential European countries, such as France and England, and accepted certain limits in the Mediterranean, allowed these countries greater freedom there. During the 17th century, new threats were developing along the imperial borders. The Persians attacked on the eastern flank, while to the north the Habsburgs of Austria attempted to extend their influence into the Balkans. Above all, the Russian czars were expressing growing territorial ambitions. The downfall of the Ottoman power took place in two phases during the reign of the great vizier Kara Moustafa. After several conflicts the Turkish sovereign had to concede to Czar Peter the Great the right to protect the Orthodox Christians in the Byzantine Empire, a relinquishment of much domestic legitimacy. He was then roundly defeated in 1683 at the siege of Vienna by a coalition of Christian armies. Spurred by this success, the allies united in a Holy League. The Turks were again beaten by the Russians, then by the Austrians before they signed the treaty of Carlowitz in which they gave up Podolia, Ukraine, Greek Morea and Hungary, nearly one-quarter of their former territory. The end of the Ottoman Empire was in sight.

*The minaret of Yesil Camii, the "Green Mosque," in Isnik,
was built in the fourteenth century by one of Murat I's viziers.*

The Modern Mediterranean

In the 18th and 19th centuries, decisive changes took place in Europe. Beginning in France, the revolutionary movements of 1789 and 1848 spread across the continent. The campaigns of the French emperor Napoleon I, the English industrial revolution, the growing rivalry among Prussia, Austria and Russia, as well as the golden age of science, the birth of the theories of capitalism and socialism all contributed to change mentalities. Old borders became obsolete. Russia took the Crimea (1783) and Bessarabia (1812) from the Ottomans and Greece declared its independence in 1822 after fighting heroically against the Turkish occupants. Shortly thereafter, war broke out between the pro-Greek coalition among the western powers (England, France and Russia) and the Ottoman Empire, resulting in the defeat of the Turkish navy at Navarin in 1829.

This defeat whetted the Europeans' colonial aspirations. Western countries introduced their cultures and technology to the southern shores of the Mediterranean. Between 1859 and 1869 Ferdinand de Lesseps, a Frenchman, built the Suez Canal, in which England was the main shareholder. This new 161-kilometer-long waterway from the Red Sea to the Mediterranean brought a revolution to merchant traffic, reducing by half the distance between the North Sea and the Persian Gulf.

While colonial empires were being built in Africa, Europe experienced two major conflicts: the Franco-German War of 1871 and the Great War or the First World War. From 1914 to 1918, the Central Powers (Prussia, Austria-Hungary, Turkey and Bulgaria) opposed a coalition of Allies, led by England, France and Russia. During the period between these two wars, while European colonialism was at its full, the inexorable decline of the Ottoman Empire began. France conquered Algeria in 1830, imposed its protectorate on Tunisia in 1881 and on Morocco in 1912, after contention with Germany in 1905. In 1908, Austria-Hungary 'trampled' Bosnia to reach the Mediterranean. A year later the Young Turks took power in Istanbul deposing the "red sultan," Abdülhamid II, an autocratic tyrant who had ruled the empire for 32 years.

Immediately upon taking power, the revolutionaries expressed their staunch opposition to Western interests; they carried out massacres of the Armenian Christian population.

In 1912 Bulgaria, Greece, Serbia and Montenegro, encouraged by the Italian's easy victory in the region around Tripoli in 1911-1912 decided to divide up Macedonia and thrace which were still in Ottoman hands. Istanbul requested aid from Europe, which refused to lift a finger in their defense. This crisis brought on the Balkan War, with its catastophic outcome for the Turks who lost Salonica, Albania, Epirus, Macedonia and much of Thrace. Their resentment was such that they immediately adopted Germany's anti-European stance. Meanwhile England, which had occupied Malta as early as 1800 and had settled in Egypt in 1882, proceeded to annex Cyprus in 1914. The horrors of the First World War did not appease the European demons. The defeat of the Prussian, Austro-Hungarian bloc brought down its allies as well; foremost among them was the Ottoman Empire. The armistice at Mudros was its death knell. The Empire was carved up and occupied by the Allies. In 1922, Mustafa Kemal abolished the sultanate, and two years later, the caliphate, to create modern Turkey.

In the Middle East, France and England divided up Syria, Lebanon and Palestine in 1916. Complications arose as the sequence of events accelerated. The Second World War broke out in 1939 between the democratic countries of Europe and America and the Axis powers, led by Hitlerite Germany. The Mediterranean became one of the principal theaters of war. The Italians under Mussolini attacked Greece in 1940, but suffered Allied reprisals. In order to save Mussolini from being crushed, Hitler intervened the following year in Sicily, then went on to attack Cyrene and invaded Yugoslavia, continental Greece and Crete. While the British were gaining control of the Middle East, another German army occupied northern France. Despite a few victories, the Axis powers were forced to give ground at the end of the year. Resistance was organized in the occupied countries and serious damage inflicted on the Germans. The American and British landings in Algeria and Morocco in 1942 signaled that the tide was turning. The Allies finally won in 1945, but it was a bitter victory. The terrible conflict had cost millions of human lives; atrocities were perpetrated that until then had been unknown to the world.

After the war, nothing could be as it had been before. The "Cold War" developed between the two principal powers, the United States and the Soviet Union, each with its respective allies. The Mediterranean became the main theater where the often-violent new world order would be played out. It received the full impact of the two main post-war political events: decolonization and the creation of the state of Israel. Colonial peoples had lost many of their sons during the world wars and no longer accepted to shed blood for far-off European mother countries that often held them in disdain. Nationalist movements had already existed in the past. In 1903, a widespread anti-French revolt had set Kabylie ablaze. Starting in 1940, however, nationalist demands turned into struggles for independence. Syria and Lebanon proclaimed their independence in 1941 and 1943, respectively. King Idris I's Libya obtained its from England and France in 1951. The latter finally granted Morocco and Tunisia their independence in 1956, while England did likewise for Cyprus in 1960. For eight years, Algerians opposed the French army in a brutal war, ending with the painful birth of an independent state in 1962. The consequences of this sanguinary encounter can still be felt in contemporary Algeria, torn apart by the pitiless struggle between partisans of the

Sunset over the Bosporus with the domes and minarets of Rüstem Pasha Camii and Sülemaniye Camii appearing in the background.

declaration of 1917 had promised them a "Jewish homeland," a vague formula aimed mainly at securing them as allies during international conflicts. Immediately thereafter, however, groups of immigrants began to settle in Israel, provoking the anger of Palestinian Arabs. At the same time and for the same reasons, on the eve of World War II, the English guaranteed a kingdom to Arab King Faysal. At the end of the war, however, this promise was not kept. Considering themselves betrayed by the West, the Palestinians, with the support of the Arab countries, entered a phase of revolt against the Judeo-Christian order imposed by the Western countries. Nothing could convince the Jews and the Arabs that they belonged to the same people and that the difference between them was only one of religion. As each party esteemed itself the rightful owner of Palestine, war was inevitable. It broke out first in 1967, as the Six-Day War. The Arab coalition was decisively beaten.

The second conflict, the Kippur War, set the region ablaze in 1973. Once again, the Arabs were defeated. In 1982, the Israeli army entered Lebanon where a fratricidal war between Christians and Muslims had been in progress since 1975. Today, in spite of multiple efforts by men of good will in both camps, the calm remains precarious. The peace process that finally began after the Camp David agreements has been blocked by the unltranationalist policy of the Israeli Prime Minister, Netanyahu. Moreover, behind the scenes, several countries, namely the Islamic nations of Iran and Sudan, continue to add fuel to the fire.

The explosive situation in the eastern Mediterranean is likely to endure because the United States, Israel's principal ally in the region, seems to lack a clear policy, especially since the collapse of the Soviet bloc. Secondly, the successive governments of western countries such as France have shown a singular lack of courage. Thirdly, Libya, Iraq, Turkey and Syria continue to engage in covert actions defending a variety of interests.

A study of the distribution of arms and wealth reveals that the old east-west Mediterranean split has given way to a new, more troubling and dangerous division between the north and the south. Hidden by religious pretexts, lies, in fact, the opposition between the rich countries of the northern shore and the poor nations of the southern shore.

revolutionary party in power and Muslim fundamentalists who want to establish an Islamic state. Finally, in 1964 Malta obtained independence from England. In Cyprus in 1974 Turkish troops, using the pretext of a pro-Greek Cypriot coup, invaded the northern third of the island and founded the Turkish Federated State of Cyprus that has existed until the present time. The island has been the scene of much bloodshed and, despite the presence of UN soldiers, there were new victims as recently as 1996.

The second powder keg is located in the Middle East and its existence is related to the creation of the religious state of Israel in 1947-1948. At the end of the Second World War the big question was whether Jews, many of whom had been in Hitler's death camps, had the right to dispose of an independent state where their forefathers had lived. The international community answered affirmatively, but, as is its habit, also secretively and ambiguously. The famous Balfour

R. Campana

THE MEDITERRANEAN PEOPLES

The Mediterranean is a violent region. It has seen the birth and death of more wars, revolutions, empires and kingdoms than any other place on earth. Today it is still the most explosive area of the world with both shores torn by fratricidal ethnic struggles and a brutal conflict among the three major revealed religions of the world. People who live there are proud and quick to take offence when their honor is challenged. They give exaggerated importance to simple everyday events. People's laughter is loud and bitter tears are easily shed. It is this surprising mixture of love and death, and of light and shadow that gives the Mediterranean soul its charm and ambiguity.

Knowing how to take one's time and enjoy life is not merely an idle saying.
As a lifestyle, it has allowed Mediterranean people, such as these Greeks from the Cyclades, to adapt to their environment.

A pretty Syrian girl from Djablah, attracted by the noise of the street. ▷

MIXED POPULATIONS AND A MELTING POT OF IDEAS

Human beings, Homo sapiens sapiens, are the heirs to a long line of Hominidae and men whose history probably began millions of years ago in east Africa. After leaving this region, known as the cradle of mankind, various groups emigrated to other continents. They suffered radical climatic variations (glacial periods followed by warming up), which caused new land passages to open leading them to unknown parts.
Modern man is the descendant of this single human ancestor, believed by specialists to have appeared in the Middle East between 400,000 and 100,000 years ago.
From there, he set out to conquer the Mediterranean basin.

IS THERE A MEDITERRANEAN "RACE"?

The term "race" is often used incorrectly. The white, yellow, black or Australoid race are terms that have fallen into disuse, for this distinction, although neutral and not unfounded as far as ethnological research is concerned, has given rise to too many racist slurs. At times, the different ethnological and cultural levels of meanings have been completely misconstrued. For example, it is ridiculous to speak of the Arab race as opposed to the white race since Arabs are Semites, members of the latter group. Using the term Jewish race is even more absurd, as the Jews do not constitute an ethnic group, but rather a religious group! Clearly and simply, there is one and only one human race. The visible differences between human groups, such as morphology, skin color and hair, were previously the bases of scientific classifications into phenotypes, but in fact are merely the result of man's adapting to his natural surroundings. These distinctive characteristics have been reinforced by environmental stability. They have slowly become part of people's genetic makeup and have been confirmed over the course of thousands of years by marriages within the same ethnic group.

This is the origin of what used to be known as the four major "races", within which could be distinguished ethnic groups and physical types. There are several human types present in the Mediterranean area. An Egyptian from the Nile delta hardly resembles a Yugoslav from the highlands. Nor does the physiognomy of a southern Spaniard coincide with that of a man from eastern Turkey.

And yet, despite all these differences, one can pinpoint several physical traits common to the Mediterranean basin which make it possible to define a human phenotype that for convenience sake can be called Mediterranean. Those who comprise this group all tend to have three or more of the following characteristics: they are relatively short, their skull is dolichocephal or long, their skin is mat, their hair is black and they have quite a lot of body hair. One frequently comes across blue-eyed blondes or redheads, however. For, if there is one uncontested primary fact, it is that Mediterranean people are of mixed ancestry. Which Mediterranean people could possibly have been able to keep its blood "pure," considering the tumultuous history of the region and the incessant exchanges and intermarriages.

The Neolithic revolution

For several thousands of years small groups of nomads from the Middle East advanced westward to both shores of the unknown and undoubtedly frightening, Mediterranean Sea. The ever-changing dangerous body of water seemed quite mysterious and they must have kept a healthy distance from its shores. Indeed, no traces whatsoever of sea craft have been found dating back further than 6,500 years, whereas the remains of river skiffs existed in Mesopotamia and Egypt nine thousand years before the Christian era. The early Mediterraneans lived from hunting, gathering and fishing. History, however, was to catch up with them. Eleven thousand years ago an event took place that resounded like a clap of thunder in Middle Eastern people's daily lives: the Neolithic "revolution." It did not happen overnight, but took over 3,000 years to be completed. The revolution was the invention of farming by the peoples of the Levant!

The region known as the Fertile Crescent includes Palestine, Lebanon, southeastern Turkey, northern Syria and Mesopotamia. The first sites of this civilization were the valleys and western slopes of the Zagros Mountains, the southeastern ranges of Turkey and the Anatolian plateau to the south. Tribes then moved on to lower lands. Groups of nomads began to settle the fertile plains. Lifestyles changed rapidly. Stone houses were built to last longer, various tools were invented, temples to different gods of the elements - the sky, earth, rain and water - were erected while a hierarchical society came into existence. These tribes cultivated wild wheat and barley and domesticated sheep,

goats and finally oxen. In fact, the bull was venerated by important bull cults, and came to symbolize virility and force throughout the eastern Mediterranean. Many fecundity cults appeared with their corteges of heavy-breasted or multiple-breasted goddesses sporting the distended bellies of pregnant women. Lastly came incredibly large cities, some holding as many as 50,000 people! Archeologists have discovered the circular foundations of the first huts in Jericho, on the west bank of the Jordan River and in Beïda in Jordan. Pottery developed about 8,500 years ago to meet the needs of domestic life and the increasing amounts of food to stock and cook.

Trade, probably based on barter, was created between the main cities. Jericho exchanged salt and bitumen for Anatolian volcanic glass, turquoise from the Sinaï and shells from the Red Sea. Catal Küyük traded its volcanic glass for Mediterranean shells and Syrian flint. On all these sites, remains of non-native objects and materials have been unearthed, thus proving that either by trade or ritual exchanges, men maintained relations across the sea and that there were already inter-ethnic marriages as far back as the early Neolithic period. Later, the advent of sea going ships increased the frequency and the number of these exchanges.

On the site of Lempa, Cyprus, reconstructed houses give an idea of what life
was like in the Chalcolithic Age (3900-2500 years BC).

A French shepherd in the Luberon region.

PASSION, VIOLENCE AND PARADOX

Jean Giono once said, "the Mediterranean is as violent as is its light." Indeed, the ancient and contemporary history of these countries has been particularly tumultuous. Today, at the end of the twentieth century, conflicts have become even more intense. One can judge for oneself. On the northern shore of the Mediterranean, Spain is under attack from the ETA, while Italy and especially France, are again the seat of independence movements prone to bloodshed and violence. Former Yugoslavia literally imploded after the terrible civil war that for several years opposed Croats, Serbs and Muslim Bosnians. Five new countries emerged, some with great suffering, from the previous federation: Slovenia, Croatia, Bosnia, Yugoslavia itself, which is composed of Serbia, Kosovo, Montenegro and Macedonia. Turkey is facing a three-sided problem. On the domestic front, a renascence of religious fundamentalism has brought to power a government with Islamic leanings. Secondly, its territorial disputes with Greece continue. The most recent conflict, in 1995, over the

sovereignty of a tiny island in the Aegean almost turned into open warfare. Lastly, its army is involved in a relentless combat to suppress the Kurdish rebellion. There is also the thorny problem of Cyprus, two-thirds of which are part of the Greek Cypriot Republic. In the northern part of the island, Turkey supports the Turkish Cypriot Republic, established with the help of its army in 1974 and still without the recognition of the international community. Over sixty thousand Turkish settlers have been sent there. Outbursts between Greek and Turkish Cypriots are common; the latest took place in 1996 and caused innumerable casualties.

The situation is even worse in the Middle East. The horrendous ten-year civil war in Lebanon left the country shattered. The wounds are such that it will take several generations before they can begin to heal. The Syrian army occupies three-quarters of the country. The South Lebanon Army and the Israeli army control the zone south of the Litani River. Sporadically, the Fatah, Hamas and Hezbollah militias, armed and supported by Syria or Iran, indicate their presence throughout the country. In Palestine, the Israeli-Palestinian conflict drags on, bringing a succession of attacks and deaths to both camps. Since the 1996 election as Israeli Prime Minister of Netanyahu, a hawk supported by conservative religious parties, both Israelis and Palestinians have adopted their homes, women must be protected from the eyes of other men, which explains the use of veils and other masks. Paradoxically, a husband is proud of his wife's beauty and expects her to wear jewelry, attractive make up and beautiful clothes, but for him alone, not for others. He likes to hear that his wife is beautiful, but does not appreciate other men

radical positions and tensions have grown. More than ever the talk of war is on everyone's lips and the sound of boots can be heard. The southern shore of the Mediterranean is hardly better off. The Egyptian government is having great difficulty controlling the sanguinary religious fanaticism of the Muslim Brotherhood. Border disputes with Libya and its unpredictable leader Quaddafi break out regularly. Algeria daily slips further into murder and anarchy. Islamic terrorists indiscriminately kill anyone suspected of collaborating with the sacrilegious West, from professors to reporters. In short, the Mediterranean is not a peaceful place.

Are there any explanations why such a radiant land with the advantages of sun and sea should be subject to such a wave of violence? There are several reasons for the apparent contradiction. The first is that the Mediterranean world is traditionally a man's universe. Family pride and an acute sense of honor are basic to society. An example is the Sicilian or Corsican custom of revenge. The second is the innate taste for paradox that motivates Mediterranean men. They speak loudly, live out of doors and like to be seen in public, yet they protect their private lives in tightly sealed houses. Algerian and Egyptian women are experts on the subject! Outside of

contemplating her. Consequently she is often veiled and forbidden to leave the family sphere. Today, fundamentalist Muslims commonly impose this practice. The Mediterranean man wants peace, but is always ready to take up arms to defend his honor, even if it means igniting the infernal round of clan vengeance and debts of honor. This paradox has always been the rule on all Mediterranean shores.

A third leit motif of the area is the permanent defiance of death. Mediterranean men like putting their lives on the line, without hesitation, out of simple pride if others are present never giving in to an adversary in public. The corrida is a perfect illustration. Bullfights are not limited to Spain or southern France; they already existed in Crete four thousand years ago. Throughout the Mediterranean world, there are numerous legends concerning bulls: an ancestor may have been a bull or there may be a marriage with a bull born of the seas or a heifer descended from the heavens. Bull cults were widespread as early as five thousand years ago, as testify the great sanctuaries in their honor. The bull is the symbol of virile strength; it will attack its enemies fearlessly until the fatal outcome. What is a bullfight if not the open fight between males for "honor" alone.

An Italian sea-faring fisherman from Taranto.
A Turkish peasant from Marmaris.
An Egyptian farmer from Sidi Barrani.
A Greek villager from Kilada.

The idea of one god came to be grafted on these cultural and psychological foundations, stirring up passions everywhere. Monotheism, or more precisely, the early monotheisms, appeared in the eastern part of the Mediterranean and in the Middle East over 3,000 years ago. Until then, existing religious

systems included various polytheistic pantheons that competed or lived side by side, but in no case denied one another. The Egyptians under Pharaoh Amenhotep IV, known as Akhenaton, were the first to break with tradition in the 14th century BC. A surprising religious syncretism developed in the middle of the 18th dynasty which united all the gods in one supreme being, a sort of "super-god", symbolized by Re-Harakhte, the sun-god, whose creative power was exalted in numerous hymns. Another name of this god was the Aton, or 'the disk of the sun.' The pharaoh Amenhotep IV was attracted to this form of nature worship, which extolled the life-giving principle and he imposed the new religion on his people, despite opposition from priests who defended the old religion. He changed his name to Akhenaton, or "One Useful to Aton" and built a new capital called "The Horizon of Aton." He proclaimed that there was only one true god, Aton, who united in love not only his Egyptian sons, but also all those who worshiped him. This first form of monotheism, however, did not survive the death of its founder.

The second monotheism that affected the Mediterranean area and brought a radical change to the very concept of gods was Judaism, born in western Palestine. The early Hebrews were the only tribe of the region that did not have a mythology, or rather, that had eliminated it in favor of one invisible and all-powerful god whom it was forbidden to portray. He resided in the temple in Jerusalem and only his priests could approach his essence in the Holy of Holies. The new god, Yahweh, or "he who is", was solitary and absolute. He did not rival any

of the other gods; he simply denied, ignored or absorbed them. This mysterious new god of the desert was a jealous god, and for the first time in the history of mankind one who demanded a definitive choice by human beings. Either they recognized him as the one and only god and would be the "chosen people" or else were against him, in which case he would take pitiless revenge and eliminate them. Furthermore, his followers were assigned the mission of eradicating, if necessary by force, the false religions wherever they could. Jewish monotheism was to give rise to two "daughter religions," Christianity and 622 years later, Islam.

Mithraism, another form of eastern monotheism, had meanwhile begun to have influence in the Mediterranean area. Mithra was originally an Iranian god of the Vedic tradition in India. His worship was shrouded in mystery and involved numerous initiation ceremonies. Mithraism was introduced in Asia Minor during the Hellenistic era three centuries BC and made many converts throughout the northern Mediterranean basin, particularly in Italy, where its high priest established headquarters on the Vatican heights. It was immediately one of Christianity's main competitors. Although both religions defended similar values, the extremely sanguinary Mithraic sacrificial practices were often found offensive. Mithraism disappeared towards the end of the second century, absorbed by its Christian rival. We know today, however, the important influence it had on Christianity, from the institution of the pope which is directly derived from that of the high priest, to the rite of communion, related to certain Mithraic initiation mysteries.

From the seventh century on, only three monotheistic religions remained in the Mediterranean area, Judaism, Christianity and Islam, and although they were all branches of one common belief, they never stopped opposing and influencing each other. This situation has prevailed to the present time. Jews, Christians and Muslims continue to define themselves in relation to and in opposition to each other. Yet, all go on culling, in the detested neighbor's religion, lessons and influences that they adapt to their own tastes. They all revere the same god whom they call by a different name. They all consider themselves to be the sons of Abraham and admit the others' prophets. They all insist, however, on their cultural differences, claiming to be most apt to serve the one god. Christians were the first to bring war to the Middle East in the name of their faith, as attested by three centuries of fighting during the Crusades. Muslims then imposed their reign of terror around the entire Mediterranean basin, while the Jews fought off first one, then the other. Nevertheless, many architectural wonders and literary masterpieces have been inspired by these same antagonistic religions! Cathedrals, mosques, basilicas, temples, tales, legends, medieval verse-chronicles, epics, novels and poems are the fruits of the tormented souls of these Mediterranean peoples. Likewise, the conflicts besieging the Mediterranean region today, from

the Israeli-Palestinian struggle to the partition of Cyprus and to the civil wars in Lebanon, Yugoslavia and Algeria, are in one way or another directly related to friction among the rival monotheistic religions. Economic, military or social problems are only side issues added to that foundation. Alas, the binding force of the Mediterranean peoples that could have and should have brought about lasting spiritual unity was not strong enough. In its place there has been a nightmare lasting for centuries.

In early spring, flocks of storks returning from Africa
rest in church bell towers in southern Spain.

Twisted style minarets are characteristic of the Sea of Marmara region in western Turkey.

◁ *Young Albanians wearing traditional costumes.*

Ready for prayer, an Orthodox Jew wearing a yarmulke on his head, tefillin on his forearm and a taleth or religious shawl over his shoulders, stops for a drink at a fountain near the Wailing Wall in Jerusalem, the remains of an ancient temple built by King Solomon in 969BC.

The old city of Jerusalem, seen from the Mount of Olives. Known as Al Quds by the Arabs, it is the holy city of the three major religions. To the left of the esplanade overlooking the Wailing Wall is the eleventh-century Al-Aqsa Mosque. To the right, the seventh-century Dome of the Rock, the oldest Muslim monument.

Two Eastern Orthodox priests. One is the bell-ringer in a Greek monastery, the other,
a superior from a monastery in the "Christian Mountain" in Syria.

◁ The interior of the cloister of the Cistercian monastery on Lerins, off the coast of Cannes.
It was an important monastic and theological center during the fifth and sixth centuries.

The luxurious Roman villa of Casale in Piazza Armerina, Sicily, was unearthed in 1950.
It contains superb mosaics, especially the fishing and sailing scenes
that illustrate the daily life of the third and fourth centuries.

This fisherman, a lover of the sea, devotes all his free time to building model boats. ▷

SAILORS ALL

Today the Mediterranean seems no larger than a lake, thanks to the speed and progress of modern means of transportation. It takes less than one hour to cross it by airplane from north to south and only four to travel from Gibraltar to Beirut. From the sky, it no longer seems to be an unlimited expanse. At sea level, however, those who live along its shores find it has lost none of its splendor and fascination. Anyone who has navigated on its waves knows how brutal the swells can be, and how dangerous and violent the squalls. Since ancient times, generations of sailors buffeting against the wind have learned this from experience. Those who are best acquainted with the sea's secrets and wrath are those who have always lived at one with the it.

M editerranean people were sailors long before they became fishermen. The distinction is worth making, for it indicates that adventure and the lure of new discoveries have always been more important than immediate profit. It is in the Mediterranean that men first ventured forth on unknown and dangerous waters. The sea has perpetually aroused their curiosity and affection. The

EPIC TIMES AND THE FASCINATION WITH TRAVELING

men of the Mediterranean world have always been avid to discover the secrets of faraway shores, even at the risk of their lives. The great myths of ancient Greece are revealing. Odysseus, or the Roman Ulysses, is perhaps the best example. Thanks to his stratagem, the proud city of Troy, located on the Aegean coast of present-day Turkey, was destroyed. After an argument with other Greek leaders, he decided to return alone to Ithaca, the beautiful island where his faithful wife Penelope and their son Telemachus awaited him. He was anxious to see them again, for the war had lasted ten years. He and his men set out in large wooden ships following at a distance the fleet of Agamemnon, the foremost Greek leader. Odysseus, however, was soon separated from them by a violent storm that blew him towards the shores of Thrace where he

proceeded to sack Ismaros, a city allied with the Trojans. He then headed southward and reached the land of the Lotus Easters, on the African coast. Only with difficulty did he leave the delights of this country. Going further north, he reached Sicily where he fought the Cyclopes. He escaped from these angry giants to the island of Aeolus, god of the winds. As Odysseus was about to depart, the god offered him a goatskin full of winds to help him navigate. Believing the bag to contain wine, the crew opened it, unleashing a storm that drove them back to the island. The god refused to accept them again, so Odysseus and his sailors set off, going where the currents led them. They landed on the island of the Laistrygones, frightening cannibals who destroyed all their ships; only Odysseus's escaped the disaster. Further north, he touched land at Aeaea, present-day Monte Circeo on the Italian peninsula, home of the enchantress Circe. After a number of adventures (the enchantress had turned his companions into swine, wolves and dogs), the Greeks were finally able to leave. When they arrived in sight of the island of the Sirens, bird-women with sharp claws who lured navigators by their magical songs and then devoured them, Odysseus stuffed his crew's ears with wax and had them attach him to the mast so he could still hear the monsters' fabulous chant. The ship sailed by and the hero became the

The inhabitants of the Isles Kerkenna,
Tunisia, use these "fishing amphoras" as traps.

The long immaculate beaches of the islands
of Chergui and Gharbi are visited solely by small fishing craft
and remain quiet havens of peace.

only man ever to have heard the songs and to remain alive. Next, he braved the Splymgades rocks, before passing through the Strait of Messina where the treacherous Scylla and Charybdis, monsters that swallowed up ships, lived. The next stop was the island of Thrinakia, where Apollo's white cattle grazed. Despite their leader's instructions, Odysseus's starving men slaughtered several oxen. The god's wrath was terrible. A tremendous storm ensued; Zeus stuck their ship with a lightning bolt and it sunk. The entire crew perished, except Odysseus, who had not touched the sacred meat. For nine days his boat drifted, until he was washed up, half-dead, on the beach of Ogygia, Calypso's island. The nymph Calypso did all she could to detain the shipwrecked hero, but to no avail: the god Hermes intervened to set him free. Odysseus built a new ship and again took to the sea. Once more, it was scuttled in a storm, this time one sent by Poseidon. Odysseus again almost drowned. He was washed ashore on the island of the Phaeacians, present-day Corfu, where the beautiful princess Nausicaa, daughter of King Alcinous, rescued him. He

regained his strength and convinced the king to provide him with a ship and crew to sail to Ithaca. After twenty years of wandering, he finally set foot on his native land. Thanks to Athena's help and the complicity of his son Telemachus, Odysseus regained his throne and his faithful wife, Penelope, after a final fierce combat. What did he do only a short time later? He again left his family ... and returned to the sea, his one true companion.

A similar voyage was to await another hero of the Trojan epic, Aeneas, the famous son of the beautiful Greek goddess Aphrodite, known as Venus to the Romans. While the city of Troy was burning at the hands of the Greeks, Aeneas escaped with a few companions, carrying his father on his back and leading his son Ascanius by the hand. An oracle had told him that his destiny was to found a new Troy further to the west, so he gathered the Trojan survivors on Ida and undertook to accomplish his mission. He successively touched at Thrace, Macedonia, Crete and Delos and after a long series of adventures, including the deaths of his father and many

The Mediterranean shores (here Greece and Turkey) abound in small shipyards where traditional crafts are kept alive.

◁   Although quite touristic, the old town of Cefalù, which was a major fishing port on the Tyrrhenian coast of Sicily until the mid-twentieth century, has managed to preserve the charm of its century-old residences.

A unique sight in the Mediterranean:
the famous fassoni from Santa Giusta, Sardinia.
These reed watercraft are strangely similar
to those used in Peru before the Spanish conquest,
and are still seen on Lake Titicaca.

companions, headed westward. Shortly thereafter, he arrived in southern Italy, and then Sicily. From there, another violent storm drove him to the shore of Carthage where Queen Dido received him royally. They fell passionately in love and only the gods' reminder that Carthage was not the new Troy convinced him to take to the sea again. Other adventures ensued, until Aeneas reached Italy and went to consult the Sibyl. The prophetess predicted new perils and had him descend into hell to see his father, Anchises, who told him where the city would be built. He followed the Italian coast northward to the mouth of the Tiber, where he entered into an alliance with Latinus, the king of Latium, who offered him the hand of his daughter Lavinia as a token of his fidelity. Another local leader, Turnus, king of the Rutulians, however, believed he had rights to the princess and declared war on Aeneas. The battle was long and the outcome uncertain. Aeneas decided to ask for help from old King Evander who, although Greek, had previously welcomed Aeneas's father, and was presently monarch of the place where Rome was later to be founded. Evander agreed to send him troops. The outcome of the war was settled by a single combat between Turnus and Aeneas, who was victorious. He was, thus, able to fulfill his destiny by succeeding both Turnus and Evander. Later Romulus, one of his descendants, founded Rome, the new Troy of the west, as the gods had foreordained. These great myths, as well as others from Syria, Cyprus and Egypt, are highly significant, revealing the continued existence of the Mediterranean tradition of traveling. From time immemorial, Mediterranean man, whatever his country or ethnic background, has had a unique relationship with the sea, based on love, fear, respect and complicity. This inbred, atavistic, even irrational instinct always prompts him further afield to explore unknown parts.

Take for example, the life story of Ibn Battutah, a 14th century Moroccan of flesh and blood, who made one of the most surprising voyages known to mankind. He left his native city Tangiers in 1325, at the age of 21, with the intention of making a pilgrimage to Mecca. He chose first an overland route. His caravan crossed Algeria, Tunisia and Libya, then arrived in Alexandria. From there he went to Arabia, visited Mecca and went on to see Iran, Iraq, Yemen and Syria. He then turned northward, crossing Anatolia, the Caucasus, and the Russian and Uzbekistan steppes, advancing as far as India where he was received by the sultan of Delhi at whose court he remained for nine years, before becoming a judge in the Maldives. He visited Bengal, the island of Ceylon, and most probably part of China. His return trip took him through Central Asia, then Egypt and finally Tangiers where in 1347 he completed his thirty-year voyage! Then what did he do? Like Odysseus, he set out again, this time for Spain and Sudan! Nor should we forget two other Mediterranean men, Marco Polo and Christopher Columbus, both fantastic explorers of far-off horizons.

One of the oldest fishing techniques in the world, "stick fishing," is still common in the Nile Delta.
Several men standing in the water beat the surface violently to head fish towards a net
that has been spread in the middle of the river.

Light and shadow
on fishing nets set out to dry.

Kalymnos sponges are reputed for their quality.

THE MYTH OF THE NURTURING SEA

Contrary to a widespread belief, the Mediterranean Sea does not abound with fish. Compared to other seas of the planet it is sorely lacking in marine life, due principally to its geomorphology. Paradoxical as it may seem, it is both too deep and too shallow. Because there is very little or no continental shelf, the sea floor drops very quickly off the coast to an average depth of 1,500 meters. Yet these littoral platforms, where the water is warmer and rich in nutrient elements and where fish can eat and hide in tall water plants, serve as reproducing grounds for species that prefer shallower waters at the start of their lives. In addition, the surface waters of the Mediterranean contain very few mineral salts and trace elements that are essential to the phytoplankton floating on the surface. It is, indeed, these algae and the planktonic microscopic animals that eat them that are the first link of the food chain and are basic to fish sustenance. In addition, the absence of deep abyssal troughs has resulted in a paucity of those species that generally prefer ocean depths.

Consequently, the Mediterranean is a sea with limited halieutic resources and has never been able to feed its people, except in ancient times when the demand was quite small. Today, for a number of reasons, including the increase in demand and the rise in pollution, fish catches are blatantly insufficient. If convincing is necessary, one need only observe an Atlantic

trawler when it enters port and its Mediterranean counterpart. The nets of the ocean-going vessel spill great quantities of large black or silver fish onto the bridge, whereas Mediterranean fishermen pile up a few crates with small brightly colored species. In fact, never in the course of history has fishing been the Mediterranean coastal dwellers' sole means of earning a living. Today even more than before, minor littoral and backcountry agriculture constitutes an indispensable economic complement. Most independent fishermen have a small plot of land they cultivate part time or have farmed for them while they are out at sea. Throughout the centuries, Mediterranean society has been dependent on income from both the land and the sea to sustain itself. Today, both sources of income are even more necessary in order to resist the attacks of the industrialized world. If one of them were to disappear, it would be the end of Mediterranean society.

Another rare primitive fishing technique, "stone fishing," seen here in the Egadi Islands.
Fish are frightened away from their hiding places under rocks and flee towards nets set in the water.

Colorful Maltese prows
are all decorated with a pair of delicately
carved and painted eyes .
This custom originated in ancient times
and supposedly allowed ships to "see,"
thus avoiding danger.

Cleaning and mending nets early in the morning in the Sicilian port of Mazara del Vallo.

Some of the most common Mediterranean species: sea bream, John Dory and red scorpion fish.

Small sea bream, sting fish, scorpion fish, serranids, white sea-bream, mackerels and boöps: just right for a good fish soup,
one of the popular western Mediterranean dishes.

*The port of Mykonos. Although it has been a fashionable tourist resort since the seventies',
it has lost none of its unusual beauty.*

*Tasty squid and cuttlefish from the Spanish Costa Brava are in great demand.
Their sales represent a large part of local incomes.*

Turkish fishermen pull in their net on the southern coast near Ovacik.

A grandfather and grandson gather oysters from the family farm in Gruissan in the Rousillon area of France.

Mediterranean markets abound in fresh species of all sorts.

Fishing: a traditional trade or an industrial activity?

One must not go so far as to depict the Mediterranean as a marine desert! Scientists have proven that at identical depths its waters contain as many species as the Atlantic. Each of these species, however, is represented by far fewer members; consequently, the total number of fish is much lower for an equal quantity of water than in the Atlantic. The real problem is the number of human mouths to feed. There are too many potential consumers: nearly 200 million, counting only the permanent residents of the coastal zone, and excluding both the inland regions of the Mediterranean countries and the multitude of peak season tourists. Two major events began threatening the survival of the Mediterranean three decades ago and must be taken into account for a full understanding of the problem: the advent of industrial fishing and pollution.

Large Italian, Spanish, and to a lesser extent Russian, fishing boats have been ruining the seabed by trawling extensively in shallow waters where large fish come to reproduce and develop. A devastating industrial procedure is the use of the purse seine, which captures en masse bonitos and anchovies all the year long. Fish with long life cycles do not have time to reconstitute their stock because of the great frequency of the catches. This phenomenon concerns deep-water pelagic or oceanic, species (such as tuna and swordfish), deep-water benthic species, (such as the scorpion fish, groupers, dolphin and sea bream) and bottom-dwelling species living between depths of 100 and 600 meters, but which often hunt on the surface (such as the hake and the whiting pout). The maximal level of exploitation of the red tuna was reached in 1994 and

As demand for fish increases, so does the size of Mediterranean catches.
Certain species, such as red tuna, have difficulty renewing their numbers.
The same threat hangs over Mediterranean bream, another common deep-water variety.

◁ Tuna fishing in the Egadi Islands. Most of the fish weigh over 100 kilograms; some reach as much as 300!

Draw net fishing is the most common form of industrial fishery in the Mediterranean basin.
Heavy tonnage boast use nets that can bring in over ten tons of fish per catch.

they are now considered an endangered species. On the other hand, fish with short life cycles that live in the upper layers, such as anchovies and sardines, can bear the impact of this type of fishing, though for how long remains debatable.

In addition, shorefront nations tend to use the Mediterranean as a dump, emptying into it 650,000 tons of petroleum and 2,500,000 tons of industrial waste each year. Mediterranean cities pour 25 million cubic meters of sewage daily into the sea! Eventually the Mediterranean will have to be protected effectively, as was recommended in the famous Action Plan for the Mediterranean published by the United Nations. The objective is not to make it an ecological museum. It is necessary, however, to restrict drastically these countries' abuse and to make them at long last understand their responsibilities. Only then, will small-scale fishing, the only sort that is viable in the Mediterranean, recover its rights. Unlike the oceans, the Mediterranean can only survive on a human scale.

Provided small-scale local fishermen are allowed to ply their traditional trade, there is room for everyone here: those who fish for swordfish in Messina or tuna off the Tunisian, Sardinian and Egyptian coasts, the sardine fishermen from Marseille or Kalamata, those who hunt for anchovies off Malta and Cyprus, red mullets off former Yugoslavia and Lebanon, sea bream in Adriatic and Ionian waters, shrimp along the Algerian and Moroccan shores, not to mention the diver who surfaces with sponges from Aegean and North African waters or coral from the submarine formations near Sardinia and Corsica. In the short run, the anarchic continuation of industrial fishing coupled with the exponential increase in various forms of pollution and the consequent depletion of species mean the death of fishing in the Mediterranean. Consequently, it signifies the end of traditional societies and their ancestral ways of life throughout area. Few Mediterranean people are willing to accept this, but they alone cannot resist the many threats.

This fish farm off the Cypriot port of Potamos Lioptriou
is the largest in the eastern Mediterranean.

CURRENT MEDITERRANEAN FISHING TECHNIQUES

Fortunately, many Mediterranean fisheries have remained small-scale, which explains the great quantity of small, low-tonnage boats dispersed among a multitude of tiny ports. During the last four decades, however, larger boats equipped with radar, sonars and immense nets have made their appearance. Total captures of fish, squid and shellfish have doubled in the last twenty years, increasing from 600,000 tons in 1955 to 1,150,000 tons in 1985. Since then, quantities have leveled off as the number of individual fish among the different species has dropped.

There are notable differences in fishing practices between the small-scale local fishermen and the commercial fishing industry. Local fishermen generally practice their trade along a narrow strip of littoral zone, between the surface and a depth of 100 meters. They use traditional techniques some of which date back to ancient times: beach seines, handlines, cast nets, harpoons, bottom lines, trammel nets, madragues or tuna nets, not to mention the rare antiquated methods such as stones and beating. These fishermen catch conger and moray, but most of all small fish dwelling in shallow waters, such as shad, anchovy, mullet, saddled bream, white bream, sardines and scorpion fish. Swordfish and large tunas can be caught with a madrague. Light-fishing is rarer and strictly regulated because of the havoc it has wreaked, particularly in anchovy and sardine catches.

Inshore or coastal fishing, which comprises over half of the catches between depths of 100 and 200 meters, extends as far as the edge of the continental shelf, where the continental slope begins. The boats used here are larger and better equipped than the preceding category. Bottom trawls and bottom lines are the most widely used techniques. Congers, sea breams, soles, sharks and rays are the most common catches. The last type of fishery is practiced on the high seas and involves sizable vessels using modern techniques including large seines, pelagic trawls, longlines and bottom set gillnets. It is carried out at two different depths. Between the surface and 300 meters catches include mostly striped-back and stripped-bottom bonitos, capelins, large swordfish, scad, sea

Like their southern Spanish counterparts, the large Moroccan fishing ports (here, al-Hoceima) have been influenced by the Atlantic culture. Their boats operate, however, in the eastern waters of the Mediterranean for much of the year.

pike and striped tuna. From 300 to1000 meters below the surface, one finds anglers, megrim, blue mackerel and hake. Here catches are less copious due to the paucity of bottom-dwellers. There are still other types of fishery widespread in the Mediterranean, involving crustaceans, mollusks, sponges and corals. The first group consists mostly of sea spiders, crabs, shrimps, lobsters, crayfish and langoustines or scampi that are gathered in the coastal zones, estuaries and the upper parts of the continental slope. Trawling, dragging, beach seines, trammel nets, and particularly lobster pots and traps are the most common equipment. Periwinkles, cockles, venus clams, clams, razor clams, cuttlefish and squid, that live along the coast on rocks and sandy beaches can be dredged or collected by hand or using a rake. Aquaculture produces the greatest quantity of oysters, mussels and clams using lagoons or large basins located close to the coast. The last type of fishery concerns sponges and corals, particularly the precious red coral from Sardinia and Corsica, which are collected by individual divers from depths as great as 100 meters.

The difficulties facing the small-scale independent fisherman trying to balance his budget arise from the general situation in the Mediterranean basin, namely the shortage of fish, pollution and human overpopulation. There is also the very specific seasonal nature of the demand here, which is both irregular and changeable. The law of supply and demand is indeed harder on the Mediterranean fisherman than on his Atlantic counterpart. His fish sell for twice as much as Atlantic fish of equal size and quantity. Apparent profits, however, are drastically limited by consumer requirements. Fashions in taste change without rhyme or reason. At present, for instance, anchovies and sardines, which represent one-third of the catch, sell badly. The size and appearance of the fish seem to be the criteria for purchase. Expensive fish such as mackerel, sea bream, red mullet and other soles that are in demand will nevertheless remain in shops if they are too small or if their exterior has been even slightly damaged. On these criteria alone one-third to one-half of many catches are thrown back to sea.

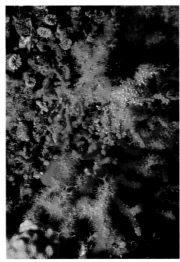

Highly valued red coral from
the Mediterranean used in jewelry making
is found off the coasts of Corsica, Sardinia
and North Africa, where divers go to a depth
of 100 meters to retrieve it.

These two photographs seem to epitomize, albeit exaggeratedly, the traditional image of the Mediterranean couple: while the woman works, her husband enjoys himself! The reality, however, is quite different!

A TWO-TIERED SOCIETY

When countries are at peace, their inhabitants can enjoy nature's benevolence. At those times, life in the Mediterranean basin is good. Nevertheless, the parameters of happiness vary considerably according to one's sex and whether or not one belongs to a Muslim society. Indeed, within Mediterranean societies, there has long existed a veritable dichotomy based on gender differences. Certain ethnic and religious groups have recently radicalized these characteristics. Generally speaking, Mediterranean women do not have the same spatio-cultural rights as their male companions. This, however, does not mean they have none. Their prerogatives are merely different and these they defend jealously.

BIRTH OF THE MEDITERRANEAN PATRIARCHY

Mediterranean society has always been patriarchal, or more precisely, patrilineal and patrilocal. In fact, filiation and social organization take into account paternal ascendance only and require that when a woman marries she leave her father's home to take up residence with her husband's family. The reason underlying all these traditions, and the choice of residence in particular, is women's weakness and their need for protection. When a father no longer assumes this responsibility, the husband, or in certain cases, the brother or the elder son does. One result of this tradition is that Mediterranean men appear as 'machos' in the eyes of Westerners.

Mediterranean man, however, did not invent patriarchal societies. The system has existed throughout the world since prehistoric times. In all primitive hunter-gatherer societies, women shared in ensuring group survival by providing most of the required food. They mastered farming and gathering techniques as well as cooking. Hunting and crafts, the more noble occupations, however, were the prerogative of men alone. Some matriarchal societies did exist, but even within them, protecting the group was men's responsibility. This historical footnote serves merely as a reminder that the existence of gender oriented tasks is part of ancient history: the outside world was man's sphere, the interior, woman's.

The Sumerians laid the foundations of patriarchies, by assigning women a set position in the male-dominated Mesopotamian society 5,000 years ago. At the same time, in Crete a more complex system was being established which, while limiting women's power within society, nevertheless granted them absolute preeminence in religious matters. They were, moreover, complete equals where civil rights were concerned. So, at one point in its history there were two diametrically opposite models in the Mediterranean world. It opted for the former. These definitive choices took place in two different locations and at two different eras. Towards the end of the second millennium BC, the Hebrew kingdoms established a society based on the belief in one unique and invisible god. This male god, however, considered women as the source of temptation and sin, even the instruments of Evil. Jewish tradition quickly made a rigid distinction between the sexes, by restricting women's place in society and confining them to the role of keepers of the hearth. This concept was to spread throughout the Middle East.

What could be more enjoyable than drinking ouzo with friends on a café terrace?
A Calabrian woman brings a glass of cool water to accompany the burning hot coffee she has just served.

The second event took place in ancient Greece. During the Golden Age of classical Greece, from the fifth to the third centuries, Hellenic society professed a frank cultural hostility to women. They were considered inferior and forced to remain at home with their young children. A special room, the gynaeceum, was reserved for them. They were not allowed to participate in public life and were held in low esteem because of their physical weakness. Greek idealization of men, the exalting of virile virtues and the common practice of male homosexuality all illustrate the cultural and political rejection of women. Rome adopted a moderate version of this model and women took a greater part in everyday life. The virtues of the *matrona*, or mistress of the hearth, were glorified, although unlimited and uncontested authority lay with the *pater familias*, and his power of life and death over all members of the family. Noble women achieved relative social importance in republican and imperial Rome, but most of their prerogatives were exercised in the shadow of their husbands or sons.

The advent of the last two monotheistic religions, Christianity and Islam, six centuries later, merely confirmed the previous status quo. Both faiths were born of Judaism and both intensified its features. Eve became the temptress, the devil's handmaiden, symbolizing the harm an intellectually and physically weak being could wreak. She was responsible for mankind's suffering on earth, and she was the source of future corruption. Under Islam, the system reached its apogee, relegating women to the rank of second-class citizens. Today, certain Sunnites and most Shi'ites impose on their wives and daughters a series of coercive customs ranging from wearing *hijabs*, *burkas* or *tchadors* to exclusion from participation in public life. Some orthodox Christian and Jewish groups, though fortunately not many, are embarking on an identical path. The growth of religious fanaticism is one of the characteristics of the end of the twentieth century. The Mediterranean basin offers an increasing number of examples of total gender-based social discrimination.

At festivities in the northern hills
of the Middle Atlas Mountains,
a group of young Berber women wearing their
traditional costumes gather in the women's quarters.

One's immediate environment is of the utmost importance;
this woman patiently repaints the cement joints of the paving stones every week.

THE PLACE OF MEN AND WOMEN IN SOCIETY

Today, the social and political situation of women is not uniform throughout the Mediterranean area. Although it is still possible to find Jewish, Christian and Muslim groups which have, in the name of their holy books, bestowed an inferior social status on their wives and daughters, most Mediterranean societies have granted women a choice position parallel to that of men. They key word, of course, is parallel, as opposed to alongside them; therein lies the nuance.

Each sex's sphere was specified and defined a long time ago: the outside world and public life for men, the interior, houses and children for women. In reality, however, distinctions are subtler. Traditionally men are the owners of the patronym, the house, the land and the family valuables. Once a woman has taken her husband's name, she becomes the guardian of that tradition, gives her husband descendants, raises children and takes on household tasks. Agricultural work and fishing are reserved for men whose physical strength makes them more fit to bear the hardship of a long day's labor in the field or to guide a ship on the capricious sea. This, however, does not prevent women from taking part in fieldwork, either by helping their husbands and brothers, or by hiring out as hands to great landowners during harvest season. One frequently sees groups of seasonal migrant laborers, often from the same village, working from one to three months far from their native region. During the summer, Calabrian women go to Sicily to harvest vegetables, women from southern Anatolia take on gathering and cutting tomatoes on the vast plantations along the Turkish coast, in September, Lebanese women from the Beirut region pick grapes in the Bekaa valley and in November and December, Moroccan and Tunisian women pick olives in France, Italy and Greece. There are innumerable examples. On their return, they not only bring home their earnings, but they are the pride of their husbands who boast of their accomplishments. They honor the family.

Honor, the key word

Mediterranean society can only be understood by bearing in mind that the basis of all the rules that govern here is honor. Man lives in accordance with or strives to improve his image in society. He must therefore appear in his best light under all circumstances. From childhood on, boys repeatedly hear that they are custodians of the family honor and that the only meaningful virtues are those of courage and defiance. Arguments and fights, more often verbal than physical, punctuate life in schoolyards. For a child, it is out of the question to give in or lose face. For adults the problem has shifted to another level, but remains entire. Games of cards, boules or backgammon are never played for fun, but for honor. It is also for honor that one dresses better, speaks louder, or buys a bigger car than one's neighbor. Honor justified banditry in Corsica, Calabria, Sardinia and Sicily until the middle of this century and it is in the name of honor that the Mafia godfathers of sad repute act. No town or city is without its saint or founding hero whose exemplary life is a source of honor for the

inhabitants who periodically pay him homage in the form of processions and offerings. Religious and political exacerbation of this honor may lead to terrible armed conflicts, as in Bosnia, Palestine or Algeria. Fortunately, most often, disagreements are merely disputes between neighbors or rival towns and are resolved after much discussion at a café terrace or on a public bench.

In these circumstances, it is understandable that the honor of women, the guardians of the clan's moral order, is of utmost importance in men's eyes. A woman symbolizes fertility and the continuation and purity of the family's "ancestral blood." She should be protected, therefore, even if against her will, from outside influences that might taint her. This results in blatant inequality between the sexes. In the Mediterranean region, a seducer is considered a Don Juan, whereas a woman in the same situation is a whore. How many times has one heard teen-age males vociferously proclaim that no woman has any worth - except his mother and his sisters.

To protect women from the danger of "contamination" men have chosen to keep them under lock and key! The ancient Canaanites and Hebrews banned women from public life. Four centuries before the modern era, the Greeks confined them to *gynaecea*. During the last century in southern Italy, Spain and the Balkans, they were only allowed out if veiled. Today, the same system, pushed to its extreme expression and justified by the supposed will of a male god, has occasioned the aberrations seen in certain Muslim countries.

To many people of the Mediterranean region, women possess specific, almost mysterious, virtues that are passionately respected. First, they are the bestowers of life, a "magical" gift if ever there was one. Secondly, they are the mistresses of life's conclusion, in that they "reign over cemeteries, where they have the privilege of going alone," as the French historian, Braudel, put it. Indeed, women prepare the dead for burial, intercede in their favor with God, mourn publicly - the ancient tradition of weepers has been perpetuated in contemporary Maghrib, Sicily, Calabria and Albania and are responsible for remaining in communion with the deceased and honoring them regularly with flowers and prayers. Last of all, they received chastity, heaven having endowed them, unlike men, with a hymen. Although this argument may bring ironic smiles as we approach the twenty-first century, it remains very important, especially on eastern and North African shores. A woman's virginity is required for a marriage to be concluded. The day after the wedding night the groom must exhibit the "proof" of his wife's defloration. Again, in the name of honor! The circle is complete. A woman's position in society has been perfectly determined. On the other hand, she reigns uncontested within her home. Many men speak loudly outside their homes and do not raise their voices once they have crossed the threshold. When a decision concerning the family or tradition must be made, the wife's influence is always decisive. In addition, as she usually outlives her husband,

A Turkish family from Germencik, not far from Aydin,
beats sunflowers to remove the oil-filled seeds.

once a widow she has an even greater aura. As a *unemama*, she dominates the entire family whose members show her great, cult-like esteem. This has led observers to remark that a Mediterranean woman is only truly free upon the death of her husband.

One must not overstate the case. Women of the western Mediterranean, at least those living on its northern shore, enjoy a legal and social status identical to that of men. Still, tradition carries its weight and few women can be found on café terraces at cocktail hour, for example.

Men dancing during the 'Id al-Fitr in the oases of northern Libya and Egypt.

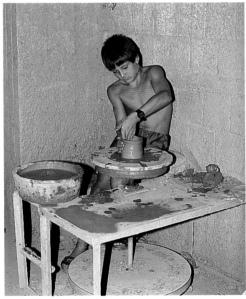

A small market-bound cart descending the sole road linking villages
of the Sinjavina Range and the city of Niksic, Montenegro.

A young boy learning ancestral pottery-making techniques in Haute Provence, France.
Traditional methods are struggling to compete with modern technology.

THE ART OF
GOOD LIVING

The superb Mediterranean countryside is a visual delight. Millions of visitors enjoy the pleasure of inhaling its perfume-scented air, swimming in its warm waters and tanning in its radiant sun. They also appreciate the local cuisine and the easy life. Yet, they only pass through; they do not settle here. They do not have time to appreciate fully the good fortune of those living along the Mediterranean shores, surrounded by beautiful countrysides. To savor the Mediterranean, one must live there all the year long, seeing it from the first pink blushes of morning, through the blinding midday sun to the magnificent red twilight. For here, the sun is the master of the house, fashioning the way of life.

The good life, here, overlooking one of the magnificent bays in the Mirambelos Gulf, northern Crete.

Primary colors and simple forms, typical of the Mediterranean region.

TYPES OF HABITATIONS

"The facade of a house resembles the face of its owner," says an Andalusian proverb. In fact, the entire house, from the door to the internal arrangement reveals the personality of those who dwell within. Even more important, it also expresses the spirit of the dominant local culture. There is not one model of Mediterranean house, just as there is not one physical type common to those living there. Each house is unique, with its distinctive features; it is its owners' pride and joy. Despite apparent differences, however, these homes all share certain common characteristics that can only be found in the Mediterranean basin and which, when united, constitute what is called the "southern style" on the septentrional shore of the sea and the "northern style" on the austral shore.

THE TROGLODYTE TRADITION AND HILLTOP VILLAGES

For many people, the term troglodyte has a prehistoric connotation, inevitably evoking images of cavemen. They are surprised to learn that there are still troglodytic dwellings in Europe, principally around the Mediterranean Sea. At first, the concepts of caves and modern life seem incompatible; yet today some people still live quite comfortably both underground and in caves excavated in mountainsides. In Matmata, in southern Tunisia, not far from the well-known island of Djerba, Berbers inhabit buried rooms at the end of large openings roughly ten meters deep dug into the ground. In Spain, in the center of Andalusia, small villages around Guadix contain numerous cave dwellings with pretty, whitewashed facades adjacent to similar hotels equipped with all the modern facilities. In southern Italy, troglodytic habitations line the walls of *scasso caveoso*, while in Turkey they abound on the south-facing Anatolian slopes that descend towards the sea. A large population of farmer-stock breeders dwells there, perpetuating its ancestral life-style. The oldest caves are used as sheep-pens or stables, whereas the larger more modern caves have been impressively decorated and equipped. In the Mediterranean zone there is a long-standing troglodytic tradition going back to Paleolithic times. Important remains have been found in Spain, Lebanon, Sicily and Cyprus. Unlike other types of primitive abodes such as huts or cabins, which disappeared over the course of centuries, cave dwellings endured. What are the reasons? The first is related to the hot dry climate of the area, where differences in temperature are considerable. The earth and rocks ensure a favorable temperature lag for every season. The second is that troglodytic habitats last as long as stone and can, therefore, be used by several successive generations without requiring costly maintenance. Lastly, in the past, this type of abode permitted its occupants to defend themselves easily once the entrance was obstructed, and this corresponds perfectly to Mediterranean people's definition of their family accommodation: a closed space.

Another typical feature of the Mediterranean landscape is the village "perched" atop a rocky hill. Houses are huddled together on the flat summit of a hill that might even have been leveled to accommodate them. The space is limited so that once the town has been built there is no possibility for growth. This explains why second villages have often been constructed at the foot of the original hilltop villages. Both old and new communities may bear the same name, differentiated only by the prefix "upper" or "lower."

The region of Guadix, Spain, where many troglodyte sites have been inhabited since prehistoric times.
The village of Purullena offers impressive examples of the whitewashed facades of homes carved in the tuff massif.

*The seven hundred odd troglodyte excavations in Matmata, Tunisia, are generally ten meters deep
and eight to twelve meters in diameter. Some are two stories high and can accommodate entire families.
A network of tunnels connects the homes with the surface.*

Mediterranean man built them as fortifications against the enemy. They are sometimes surrounded by high stone walls or built flush with the rock cliffs, thus guaranteeing their inaccessibility. The countryside of Catalonia, Castille, Provence, Liguria, Calabria and Thessaly on the north shore and the highlands of the Rif, the Middle Atlas, the Aures, the Djurdjura, and the Medjerda to the south abound with them. Everywhere, clustered habitations predominate. Mediterranean people do not like to live alone. For defensive reasons, throughout history, they have always preferred the company of their fellows. Within these built-up areas, however, there appeared a social and spatial distinction based on nobility and ancestry. In every small traditional Mediterranean village, as in every town, there is a "rich" quarter and another "working class" quarter where people of the same social group gather. The possession of traditional water rights often imposes this division. Certain families have inherited springs and sell the use of the water to farmers. This custom still exists in the eastern Mediterranean and in certain more traditional parts of the west, such as Calabria and Epirus.

The hillsides of the Djurdjura Mountains in Algeria are covered with flowers that enliven otherwise austere villages perched along the ridgelines.

Contemplating the unusual beauty of the small Corsican village of Ogliastro, one forgets that this site was selected solely for its defensive position.

*View of "Little Venice," the old quarter of Mykonos, where white houses
with colorful doors and shutters practically dip "their feet in the water."*

◁ *The town of Monemvassia in the Peloponnese, is dominated by Goula, the fortified Frankish castle, and surrounded by
sixteenth-century Turkish walls. It illustrates the Mediterranean peoples' constant concern for protection.*

The port of Bizerte was one of the most important of northern Tunisia. The entrance channel, dominated by an old fort, leads to the fishing port and the casbah, the traditional North African city, built between the thirteenth and seventeenth centuries.

SIMPLE FORMS

Despite their obvious differences, the external aspect of Mediterranean houses is regulated by the use of simple geometrical shapes: squares, cones and circles. The basic unit is the square and its natural deformation, the rectangle. Regardless of the building materials, most of the homes can be seen as the juxtaposition of square and rectangular units. The refinement involved in this juxtaposition often reflects the richness of the culture. The exterior may be softened by curves as in Spain, the western Maghrib and Greece, or adorned with annexes of varied forms, as in Malta, Yugoslavia and Turkey, or may be reduced to a simple room with a single opening, as in the eastern Maghrib, Sicily and the Napolitan *bassi*. Even when the house has several stories, as do country farms in Provence and Campania, the basic principle of the square foundation remains.

In certain regions, such as the Italian Pouilles or northwestern Syria, conical roofs of slate or gray roofing stone cover circular, often whitewashed stone homes, sometimes with a totem or religious symbol at the peak. In Syria, the shape of houses is even more surprising. They form a single cone with adobe or dry-mud walls that bulge slightly from the ground to mid-height to afford a larger interior space. In some houses, only the roof is circular in shape, while in others, the top floor of the house may be circular, as is the southern Tunisian *ghorfa*. Single cone houses may become large abodes when the cones are built side by side in a cluster of units that communicate through low doors. These are prevalent in regions with large plantations that unite extended families under the same roof. The circle is, nevertheless, rarely used as an external element. Traditionally the floor plan of a house is represented by the more austere square. On the other hand, Mediterranean people throughout the ages have enjoyed using circles for the interior arrangement and decoration of their homes, since "round forms" bring to mind warmth and fantasy. Does not the word "roundness" evoke the typically feminine world of charm and intimacy? The external aspect of the walls, thus, indicates

*There is a strange resemblance between the trulli found in the Italian Puglia region
(here Alberobello) and the "bee-hive houses" of As Sfirah in Syria.
The origin of their shape goes back to time immemorial.*

male seriousness, while the "fullness" inside suggests feminine grace. The fountains, the disposition of flower beds, the garden's floral compositions, the presence of bulging fireplaces, the partitions and the rounded upper frames of doors all reflect this. One must certainly also consider that these forms are carryovers of ancient cultural practices - altars used to be circular - as well as indications of the need to gather all clan members without regard for social rank around the home's spiritual center. Traditionally, interiors are usually sober. Their austerity is often attenuated, however, by elaborate decorations, such as the colorful tiled wainscoting in Spain, North Africa and Turkey.

The common sight of white houses descending towards the sea and blue and red cupolas of the innumerable chapels and churches is typical of housing in the Greek islands.

Formerly a common sight in the eastern Mediterranean, wooden houses have now practically disappeared. The sole survivors are in western Turkey, especially in Üslüdar and Izmit, along the northeastern shore of the Sea of Marmara.

NATURAL MATERIALS AND COLORS

Nowhere else in industrialized countries are natural materials so widely used for house construction and property improvement as in the Mediterranean basin. Stones, omnipresent on the rocky *garrigue* terrain, are commonly employed. Wood and thatch are also popular.

Stones are used for the sturdy thick walls that protect houses against the heat. They are also the sole component in the dry stone walls, which are generally no more than one meter high. Weaving across fields and terraces, patiently constructed generations ago, these walls are the "calling cards" of the region. As the ubiquitous mark of the Mediterranean countryside, they indicate orchard and property boundaries, serve as retaining walls on rocky hillsides, hold stable otherwise loose ground and border dusty paths. They are virtually identical, whether in Andalusia, Provence, Attica, Sicily, Crete and Cyprus or in Turkey, Syria, Lebanon and the Maghrib.

Wood, the quintessential noble material, has unfortunately become rare after centuries of deforestation caused either by fire or by man's anarchical logging practices. Wood is used in the construction of roof and window frames, but most importantly for doors, which if made of another material would not be worthy of the name. Wood and wood by-products are also employed extensively in interior decoration, for furniture, movable panels or decorative elements. Thatch, formerly the most common roofing material, is now reserved for luxury homes. It still covers some Camargue farmhouses, Italian *trulli* and the country homes of wealthy Greek and Spanish property owners, as well as a few farms in Sardinia and Malta. Elsewhere it has practically disappeared. It deteriorates quickly from rain and needs replacing regularly. Maintaining both the thatch and the roof frame is expensive, and the costly care it requires is beyond most people's means.

Façade colors echo those found in nature, especially the whites and blues apparent everywhere around the Mediterranean where almost two-thirds of the tints belong to these two color ranges. Everything seems to have been tuned up for a

*Mediterranean houses are generally not too large,
with small openings only to protect them from the heat and the wind.
White facades reflect the sun's rays and are often decorated with colorful flowers.*

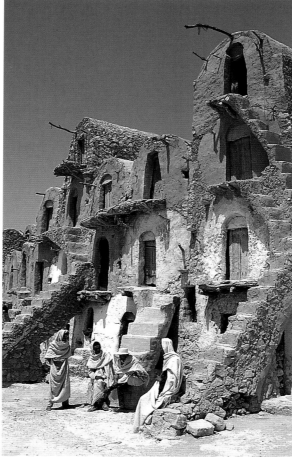

symphony in blue and white: blue white-crested waves, blue skies with white cotton clouds and blue shutters and doors against immaculate brightly whitewashed facades. The association of white and blue is *de rigueur* for private homes as well as entire towns on the coast and small islands. In this respect, a visit to the Aegean and Ionian Islands is always a delight to the eyes. The colors seem to combine in a joyous song of love of nature.

As one goes further inland, cameos of ochre, brown and pinkish-red appear, like reproductions of nature. Each region has its own traditional colors. For example, the red facades of

the Venetian islands, Sicily and Sardinia contrast with the ochres of Greece, Malta and Syria. The bluish and light-violet walls of Tunisia and Egypt answer the beige and light-brown facades of Corsica and southern Turkey. Originally, all these colors came from pigments found in clay and rocks. The time-consuming traditional techniques for extracting them are no longer cost-efficient and have become obsolete. Again, only the wealthy can afford the old style hues. Others must be satisfied with modern pigments, although manufactures have made great efforts to commercialize paints that respect the "natural tones" of the traditional facades, doors and walls.

*A ghorfa, a characteristic home in the Medenine region of southeastern Tunisia.
Bedouins used these strange alveolar-shaped buildings as granaries
until nomadic life became less common and they took to living in them.*

*The unusual architecture of Maltese cities
allies monumental Italian baroque taste with British austerity.*

*The farther east one goes in the Mediterranean basin,
the greater the contrast between the colors
of the houses and the austere, generally black,
dress of the elderly women.*

*Several regional styles using local materials have developed in southern France.
Here, houses in Martigues painted with the natural pigments of the region and farmhouses in the Camargue,
a marshland where broom thrives.*

A typical landscape of the Crété region of Tuscany. Cypresses planted as windbreaks bound fields
in which large farmhouses like French bastides stand aloof.

◁ Centuri, northwest of Cap Corsica. The general aspect of the village with its massive houses
and stone roofs has remained unaltered since the beginning of the century.

◁ The famous Ponte Vecchio over the Arno is the oldest bridge in Florence. It was built during Roman times,
destroyed and reconstructed in 1177, destroyed again in 1333 and rebuilt and enlarged for the third time in 1345
when Florentines lined both sides of the bridge with shops and back-shops that serve as homes.

A Provencal farmer braids garlic in front of his massive oak door.

Inhabitants often hang long tapestries before their doors to ward off the intense heat. ▷

DOORS AND GARDENS

The public domain has an important place in the everyday life of Mediterranean people.
Sitting at café terraces and sipping tea or cool beverages, men comment on the week's political and sports events.
Amid loud exclamations and laughter, they transform the world. Meanwhile, women exchange the latest news at
the fountain or public washhouse, chat between chores, sitting in a circle in the shade of a hedge or in front
of a house stoop. Their tone is always friendly and familiar. However, this noisy, pleasant public life stops
at the front door of each person's home; inside begins the realm of the family,
characterized by extreme discretion and sheltered from outside influences.
Mediterraneans are secretive people and very protective of their privacy.

THRESHOLDS AND DOORS

The Mediterranean house is a closed universe, uniting and sheltering the family clan under one roof. The width of the walls and the small door and window openings serve to keep out external influences as well as the heat of the day. They are obvious signs of the male need to insulate the household. Moreover, it is fascinating to observe the contrast between the bright sunlight outside and the soft shadows within the somber homes. For two to three thousand years, women have continued to whitewash the interior walls and men to render the exterior walls. Why are homes shrouded in such mystery? Again, it is a question of family honor. Wives' and daughters' virtue and obedience are not the only reflections of the family's honor. It is also represented by the family possessions, including furniture, silver and traditions, with which outsiders are not supposed to be familiar. The superficial image of the outgoing sociable Mediterranean man is misleading. He does not welcome strangers in his private domain. The room known as the *majlis* in a Muslim home was designed for entertaining male strangers and although it lies within the perimeter of the house, is located in front of the threshold itself. It is therefore rather an annex where, for example, it is not necessary to take off one's shoes, whereas etiquette requires one to remove them before entering the family area itself. Thresholds have been considered sacred since ancient times. For thousands of years building a home was carried out according to strict propitiatory rituals. Important gods and long-lost ancestors were consulted and had to give their approval. The sanctified area was off bounds to many. The Greek *gynaceum* and the Muslim harem are both examples of the concept of a private family area blessed by a divinity and destined to remain untainted by outside contamination. Thresholds were important in that they magically guard entrances and protect households from the forces of evil. These forces are the outside world, in other words the enemy, temptation and fault! Many traditions we tend to judge as folklore derive from this conception. One is the custom of the groom carrying his bride across the threshold. Another is the guest having access to certain rooms only after he has given his host a gift, while still other rooms, generally considered the women's sphere, remain off limits.

Within this context entrances play an essential role in a Mediterranean house. They traditionally open towards the east where the sun rises, symbolizing the renewal of life, and they have a twofold function. A door must exhibit to the outside world the owner's wealth and good taste, while acting

as a barrier before the threshold. The interior side of a Mediterranean door, whether it is made of wood or iron, is sober; without unnecessary embellishments. The colors are generally dark, in accord with the intimate atmosphere of the home. The exterior side, on the contrary, displays a profusion of bright blues, reds and yellows. Round or cast iron nails in geometrical patterns, flowers, stylized animals, perhaps even panels exhibiting the owners' portraits may

decorate the street side of a door. The dwelling places of the wealthy often have impeccably shined handles and knockers that enhance the beauty of the perfectly polished wooden doors. The family coat of arms, or religious or mythological characters, may decorate the doorjambs and ornamental facades. Occasionally Greek or Roman style columns frame the door. Everything is calculated to suggest to both friends and strangers that behind the door need and shabbiness are unknown.

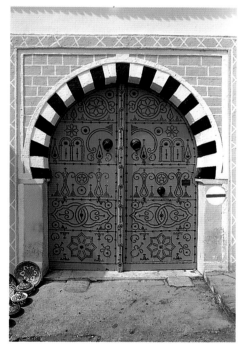

Mediterranean doors show an infinite variety of styles and decorations, from the pronounced British look of this Maltese door to the clear Arab influence of the Tunisian door.

A superb interior court in Sidi Bou Saïd, the charming Tunisian town to which artists flock.

Through a half-opened door one imagines the calm interior garden of this Naxos home.

The allure of this Maltese gentleman's residence, now partially restored as a museum, reminds one of Iberian homes.

Sheltered from the sun by high garden walls, these Cypriot women from Lefkara embroider the famous lefkaritika on tablemats.
This handicraft is quite old, as Leonardo da Vinci is known to have brought
a similar tablemat back to Italy in the fifteenth century.

THE ART OF INTERIOR GARDENS

Every Mediterranean home possesses an interior garden. Whether big or small, it is always cool, restful and sheltered from curious eyes. Here, members of the household gather to enjoy each other's company. Gardens brighten up the house by introducing natural greenery. Once the simplicity of square architectural forms gave way to more complex structures, space for a fountain was included and around it a garden with flowers, sunlight and a shady corner. This type of organization already existed in ancient Mesopotamia, Egypt and Phoenicia. The Greeks and then the Romans developed it to perfection. During the Median Wars, the Greeks discovered the beautiful gardens hidden within the great Persian homes. These *paitidaiza*, as they were called, so impressed them that they adopted a Hellenized form of the word, *paradeisos*, which became *paradis* in French, paradise in English. The Roman atrium was the center of the family abode. It was a sheltered interior court, organized around a fountain or a basin, where rich patricians planted bushes and flowerbeds. Under the Arab influence, gardens were decorated with earthenware, works of art, fruit trees, rare flowers and birdcages.

Today the inhabitants of all countries with a Mediterranean shoreline are experts in the art of gardening, each country adapting the art to its national spirit. In Spain Andalusian patios rival those of the Balearic Islands. In prestigious contests owners compete for the desirable title of 'best gardener of the year.' The small charming gardens of Myconos, Fira and Rhodes in the Greek Islands are authentic gems requiring daily care. French Provencals and Italian Tuscans are fond of

*Mediterranean houses, whether on the European or African shore,
always separate the public part of the home from the private part either by a court or a series of vestibules.*

drinking coffee or reading the newspaper in the shade of trees surrounding their cabins or *casas*. Most important, however, the garden is where one takes advantage of the cool of the evening. Barbecues, followed by discussions among friends and relatives, go on late into the night.

One specific characteristic concerns only Muslim societies: the separation between the sexes is absolute and has led to the creation of two sorts of interior courts. The first are those like the *majlis*. They open onto the outside world, in that,

like the door, they must show the visitor the master of the house's wealth. They are relatively large and carefully organized. Courts located in the very heart of the house, on the other hand, are smaller and simpler, but are in no way inferior to the *majlis* in beauty.

The women of the household are in charge here and demonstrate their good taste and finesse. When they wish to honor a guest, they present him with flowers they have picked in the inner court.

A patio in Cordoba. Southern Spanish interior courts, and especially those of Andalusia, are of such great importance to the inhabitants that each year a prestigious contest is held to select the most beautiful one.

The frequent lack of water in Corsica explains why each house possesses cisterns for the domestic water supply and basins for watering the garden.

Fetching water is a twice-daily task for this Syrian from Manbij. ▷

FRESH WATER WHIMS

Without fresh water life could not exist.
Because of the Mediterranean region's recurrent summer droughts and substantial agricultural needs,
water has long been the focus of man's attention.
At no time in history has there been enough of it.
From ancient times onward Mediterranean civilizations have suffered from the scarcity and the irregularity of
fresh water resources. The end of the twentieth century has seen tensions crystallize
over the possession of vital rivers and springs.

The hydroclimatic characteristics of the Mediterranean basin are distinctive, representing a middle ground between temperate and desert climates. The principal rainy season is the autumn followed by a minor one in spring. Summers are hot and dry and rainfall is irregular. Certain regions have been known to suffer several years of continuous drought, only to experience two or three consecutive seasons of torrential precipitation causing flash floods that devastate the local economy, as in the catastrophes that hit southern France between 1994 and 1996. In addition, summer heat and the resulting evaporation cause conditions similar to those of semi-arid zones. Farming that depends solely on rainfall is an uncertain undertaking and river water must be harnessed for the population to survive Because of the existence of many island chains, particularly in the west, notably in the Aegean and Ionian Seas, as well as the fact that the rugged relief has produced small hydrographic structures, the region possesses few large river basins. If one excludes the Nile, of which only 144,000 km2 out of the total 2,870,000 km2 are actually part of the Mediterranean area, the total surface of the 21 catchment areas is less than 800,000 km2. The eleven main drainage basins, the Asi-Oronte, the

THE CONJUNCTION OF CLIMATE, GEOLOGY AND HUMAN ACTIVITIES

Axios-Vardar, the Bûyûk-Menderes, the Ceyhan, the Cheliff, the Ebre, the Meric-Evros-Ergene, the Medjerda, the Po and the Rhone, together represent only 530,000 km2. This is very little compared to the agricultural requirements for feeding a coastal population of 140 million, plus another 200 million if one includes the entire Mediterranean basin. In addition, the number of city-dwellers there is expected to triple by the year 2025! Since underground water reserves are quite small - the biggest, those of the Ebre, the Po and the Rhone do not exceed a few dozen square kilometers - the problem of fresh water is becoming increasingly crucial each year.

Nevertheless, the situation is not identical around the entire perimeter of the Mediterranean Sea. The loss of river water due to evaporation and to human consumption illustrates the blatant disparity between north shore and south shore countries. The southern river discharge supplies only 5% of the sea's capacity, whereas the northern rivers supply 95%. One notices a similar imbalance concerning rainwater input: the north contributes an estimated 4,700 mm per square kilometer per year, while the input figure is only 811 mm from the southern countries.

Lastly, the considerable impact of man himsélf is far from

In the Maghrib (here in Chegga, Algeria) "combs" allow water to be distributed equitably
in proportion to the surface each landowner needs to irrigate.

negligible. Over the centuries he has thoughtlessly cleared the mountains of trees, modifying the ecological milieu. In many places, the thick forests of conifers and indeciduous trees that covered the mountains have completely disappeared and bushes and thickets have taken their place. Rocky terrain and loose ground without roots to retain them tend to slide away; the soil loses its fertility as it dries and groundwater levels drop. The water deficiency ineluctably increases as the growing scarcity of vegetation leads to a decrease in rainfall. This in turn causes a drop in underground and river water levels, which then induces a reduction in the vegetation. The cycle is ready to begin again.

*Despite the pollution of the Nile Delta and River as far inland as Middle Egypt,
it is the villagers' only regular source of water.*

◁ *The remarkable underground distribution network visible in the ruins of Kourion, Cyprus, show how advanced the urban
irrigation system was during the early centuries of the Common Era.*

*The Libyan coast, flanked by its omnipresent desert,
is frequently confronted with the problem of a potable water supply.
Most often, villagers have to make do with brackish water,
as in the sabkhah in Tawurgha.*

THE AGE OLD ART OF IRRIGATION

Fresh water having always been rare and precious, Mediterranean man has, since ancient times, shown great ingenuity in conserving, channeling and exploiting it. Six thousand years ago, the Syrians and Egyptians had already created complex irrigation systems and invented the first dams. In the middle of the second millennium before our era, the Greeks were quite capable of catching rainwater and creating diversions for better use of rivers and streams. The Etruscans and later the Romans perfected these methods in Italy. In the eighth century the Arabs introduced new procedures that were revolutionary at the time, such as digging long canals inspired by the Arabian *falaj*, employing systematic drainage, and finally farming marshes and flooded lands. Many ancestral techniques are still used today, such as channeling and controlling runoff, collecting rainwater directly, constructing underground buried storage reservoirs and digging drainage galleries.

Agriculture is the main consumer of fresh water. With the exception of France and Yugoslavia, each of which draws upon less than 15% of the total volume of its water resources, the needs of the Mediterranean countries are considerable. North shore countries use an average of 62% of their resources, while those of the south shore consume 93%. Two countries alone, Italy and Egypt consume 68% of all the water used for agriculture in the region.

Still another factor contributes to the imbalance in water supplies besetting the region. During the warmest months of the year, from June to September, fresh water resources decline naturally. During the same period, over 110 million tourists seeking sun and blue waters swarm to the coasts. Today the Mediterranean is already unable to satisfy this sudden seasonal rise in the demand for water and continue to respect hygiene standards. What then will the future bring?

During the last two decades the number of conflicts over the

ownership of fresh water resources has risen. Historians even speak of "water wars." All the important clashes in the southern and eastern parts of the Mediterranean are in one way or another related to the question of fresh water. Iraq and Syria watch anxiously as the flow of the Euphrates, the true lifeblood of these two countries, diminishes radically with the construction of the giant Turkish Ataturk dam on the river's upper course. Fighting has also broken out between Turkish and Syrian soldiers under various pretexts. Another example also comes from the Middle East. It is obvious that the Israeli occupation of southern Lebanon and northeastern part of the West Bank is directly linked to control over the Litani and Yarmuk Rivers. Nearly 80% of the waters of the latter are already diverted to Israel. Along the African coast, ownership of the vast subterranean water-bearing beds is the object of a fierce if silent struggle between Egypt and Libya to the east and between Libya and Tunisia to the west. Other similar and heretofore peaceful encounters have sporadically opposed Greece to Turkey and Albania. If the Mediterranean states do not soon draw up a charter for water, the likelihood of conflicts will increase and the overall situation in the Mediterranean basin will become explosive.

There were many large paddlewheels around the Mediterranean during the Middle Ages.
Although few remain in the west, one of the most interesting ones is in Cordoba on the Guadalquivir.

Modern technical contributions

Different fields of science have brought new, if partial answers to the challenges of the twentieth century. Foremost among the technical advances is the possibility to master and develop various hydrographic resources. Many large dams with deep reservoirs have been constructed and treatment to conserve water purity is being carried out at the catchment site. Meteorology is becoming an exact science thanks to information supplied by radar and geostationary satellites. More precise weather forecasts have made it possible to adjust river and underground water management to farming requirements more satisfactorily. Predictions of weather changes help farmers to accommodate their production to climatic conditions, either by partially limiting the negative effects or by amplifying the advantageous effects.

Water conservation is fundamental in the struggle to eliminate droughts that plague the Mediterranean basin. Fortunately, remarkable new techniques have been developed to make this possible. We now know how to prevent the silting up of dam reservoirs and if necessary how to unsilt them. Many important Mediterranean countries, such as Spain, France, Italy and to a lesser extent Greece and Turkey, protect river banks against erosion, maintain the quality of the soil and

systematically replant when vegetation has been destroyed. With the help of precise drilling techniques it has become possible to tap very deep underground water. The catchment and storage of groundwater in natural geological formations, such as the numerous Mediterranean coastal karsts, is another new technique. Other twentieth century inventions include the construction of long dikes along the coasts and before cove entrances in order to create stream and river-fed reservoirs, the use of desalinization techniques, the recycling of waste water, greater control of drainage and transport procedures and rational water conservation schemes. It remains to be seen whether these new techniques will complement the centuries-old traditional methods used throughout the Mediterranean zone. They may replace them altogether. Is peaceful coexistence between traditional and the modern techniques possible or will they enter into conflict? Ideally, these rigorous modern scientific procedures should come to the assistance of the ancient time-honored practices cherished by the Mediterranean peoples without destroying them. The coming twenty years will undoubtedly bring us the final answer. Mediterranean farming in its entirety depends upon it.

An excellent example of a Seljuk bridge, built in the eleventh century near Aspendos, Turkey. The Seljuks were particularly concerned by the problem of water supply and became expert in the construction of bridges and aqueducts.

◁ *This famous fountain in Spili, Crete, was already in use during ancient times and was reconstructed more than once.*

Several ingredients and spices that will season and enhance northern Maghrib dishes.

Golden virgin olive oil of French picholines flow into a bottle immediately following the first cold pressing. ▷

THE MEDITERRANEAN CUISINE

"Strange and spicy", was Lord Carrington's reaction to Mediterranean food when he first tasted tabouli. For non-Mediterraneans this cuisine offers a surprising mixture of strong exotic tastes. Natives of the area, of course, think it is the best in the world. There is no lack of sayings boasting that Mediterranean food is responsible for the longevity of the inhabitants. Whether this is pure fancy remains to be seen. Modern medicine now recommends the famous 'Cretan' diet based on olive oil, vegetables, fruit, bread and fish for all those who are concerned about their health. Over the course of the centuries there have been many different variations of the Neolithic trilogy of olives, wheat and grapes, which is still the basis of contemporary Mediterranean cooking.

DOES A MEDITERRANEAN CUISINE EXIST?

The question is worth asking, since so many African, European, Asian and Middle Eastern cultures exist among the numerous ethnic groups living along the Mediterranean shoreline. The similarities of climate and history have, however, greatly attenuated certain differences. Climatic conditions have always favored the growth of the olive-wheat-grape trinity. Despite numerous conflicts, trade between the coastal groups never ceased, thus preserving an authentic Mediterranean cultural identity. All these peoples have maintained a special relationship with nature. They quickly 'tamed' wild plants and trees and rendered them amenable to farming techniques. Since then, the smallest of these species have been grown in gardens and the largest in orchards or fields. Mediterranean man has a particular fondness for native plants. Thanks to secrets passed on from father to son, he knows which aromatic shoots to pick in the *garrigues* and scrub lands to season both the scarce game he hunts and the fish he consumes in great quantity.

All of these foods can be seen displayed in the noisy, brightly colored markets that give character to Mediterranean towns and villages. Olive oil naturally remains the basis of every Mediterranean dish, the essential ingredient that gives the local cuisine its unique and distinguishing savor. Mediterranean food is always prepared with great care. Aside from certain fast foods, such as pizzas or spaghetti, most culinary exercises require time and a healthy dose of love on the part of the cook, an occupation generally reserved for women. Preparing meals may be time consuming, but table companions show their appreciation by spending hours sharing it. A truly successful Mediterranean meal must also be an important social interlude when friends and family gather around a table, the occasion for great conviviality and lengthy conversations. Savory dishes appear in an order that respects ancestral rituals, so that each taste lastingly impregnates the palate before the next course is served. Mixing the four main savors-salt, sweet, bitter and sour - is rare and the choice is always made with care. Generally, a particular wine is associated with the main dish, to bring out the innate flavors of the ingredients. The 'fast food' fashion has only caught on in large Mediterranean cities where insipid frozen food has become the fare of a 'neutral' rushed clientele that has lost its sense of identity.

One can, therefore, speak of Mediterranean cooking in the broadest sense of the term, to the extent that common culinary practices and tastes exist throughout the Mediterranean basin. Climate and history together account for this. Both shores

of the Mediterranean are bathed in light and enjoy mild temperatures year round. Vegetation is almost identical everywhere, and consequently ingredients are surprising homogeneous. In addition, Mediterranean peoples have been trading and exchanging with each other since ancient times and have developed common gustatory and olfactory inclinations. No local cuisine could remain impervious to that of its neighbors. On the contrary, each has been enriched by foreign contributions while its own features have been accentuated. The many regional specialties are, in fact, all varied nuances of a single palate. There are, nevertheless, two distinct zones of culinary traditions: the western, or more precisely, the northern, shore of the Mediterranean and the eastern, extending from the Middle East to North Africa. Both traditions, however, are present in the intermediate area composed of the long string of islands stretching from Sicily to Malta, Crete and Cyprus, where tastes vary, some favoring the oriental tradition, others, western culinary arts.

WESTERN TASTE

In the west, Spanish cooking is uncontestably the most sophisticated and refined. Ever since the end of the Middle Ages, it has enjoyed the outstanding reputation it acquired in the courts of Europe. During the seven hundred years of Moorish occupation, it underwent strong oriental and North African influences, which explains, for example, the common Spanish use of cumin, saffron and nutmeg. The three dishes that best symbolize the Iberian culinary tradition are *paella*, now the national dish, sardines in olive oil (a marinade accompanied by vegetables) and *gazpacho*, the popular Andalusian soup. The cuisine of Mediterranean France is simpler, heartier and more rustic. Thyme, rosemary, bay leaves and above all garlic, known as the 'Provencal truffle,' are widely employed. The most well known dishes are *bouillabaisse*, a fish stew from Marseille and Corsica, cod *brandade*, *tapenade* or olive paste, and *pistou* soup from Nice, a thick vegetable soup flavored with sweet basil.

As one travels along the French coast, one begins to encounter Italian tastes. Although many people think of Italy as solely the land of pasta and pizza, it is, nevertheless, the homeland of the greatest variety of recipes in the Mediterranean. Before the 19th century and the creation of the Italian nation, Italy consisted of a series of small independent states, each developing its particular strengths in the sphere of its choice, notably that of cooking. This explains the exceptional diversity of Italian dishes most of whose main ingredients are vegetables,

fruit and fish. The most famous dishes include, black rice with cuttlefish, anchovy or sardine omelets, rabbit with olives and stuffed sardines. The Italian islands, particularly Sardinia and Sicily, offer a great variety of sheep cheeses.

Albanian and Yugoslavian food does not present any specific characteristics, since the population includes several ethnic groups of both Christian and Muslim faiths with very dissimilar customs: Slovenians, Croatians, Serbs, Bosnians, Macedonians and Albanians. One can, nevertheless, make a distinction between the west, where cottage cheese, specifically a salty cheese called *kajmak*, and cereals are the basis of the local daily fare and the principal dishes are stuffed cabbage, meatballs with yogurt and barley soup and the east where Turkish and Greek influences are evident. Here typical dishes are *imam baildi*, an eggplant dish, *tarator*, creamed cucumbers with garlic

and hot peppers, and a number of dishes using stuffed onions, spices and olive oil. Many foreigners consider Greek cooking to be the most typical of the Mediterranean region.

It is known for its consistently fresh ingredients and simple recipes incorporating a considerable variety of sea fish, shellfish and mollusk. Butter is not used at all. Greek cooks are known for their great patience; traditional dishes simmer longer here than elsewhere around the Mediterranean.

Unusual wines, such as the pine resin-tasting *retsina* and a sulfur-tasting wine accompany specialties with tempting names such as *mussaka* (stuffed eggplant), *mithi pilafi* (pilaf rice with mussels), *kalamarakia yemista* (cuttlefish stuffed with spinach), *psaria plaki* (fish in tomato sauce), *taropita* (cheese in pastry shell), *tzatziki* (creamed cucumber with mint) and *horiatiki* (tomato and cheese salad).

Onions, pimentos, garlic, various herbs and of course, olive oil are essential ingredients in Mediterranean cooking. Brissaouda consists of dipping a garlic crouton in oil and is considered a treat in the backcountry of Nice.

Some western Mediterranean dishes: fried squid from France, paella from Spain, pizza and various sorts of pasta from Italy.

EASTERN AND AFRICAN TASTE

Widespread acceptance of the Muslim cultural tradition followed in the path of the Arab conquests. In the Middle Eastern and southern shore countries, a certain uniformity

There are certain tastes found in everyday dishes that are common to the entire region, from Morocco to Turkey. People in the southern and eastern basin of the

of culinary customs is apparent. Pork, for instance, which is quite appreciated by non-Muslims to the north, is never employed. Likewise, wines and alcoholic beverages used to flavor sauces and deserts in the north are prohibited in the south. On the other hand, spices rare in the west are widely employed. At times, their presence is so dominant that the food is difficult to digest for one unfamiliar with them. Almonds, pistachios, sugar and rice are quite common. This vast Afro-oriental zone in fact begins in Turkey, which because of the Muslim religion is considered part of the eastern sphere. Each country has its specialty. There is Turkish pilaf rice and *baklawa*, a flaky pastry with honey, Syrian *tahini* or sesame paste, Israeli stuffed carp, Lebanese *tabouli* or semolina salad with tomatoes, cucumbers and mint, Egyptian *falafel* or chick pea and vegetable paddies, Libyan *harira* or lentil soup, Tunisian or Algerian *couscous* and Moroccan *tajine* or chicken with prunes. Special mention must be made of Morocco, where the refinement and the richness of the food are the equivalent of those of Spain to western cooking.

Mediterranean are fond of strongly contrasting tastes, such as sweet and sour, grilled or braised meat, sweets, fruit, spices and strong aromas. These refined culinary combinations have produced some very distinctive dishes, for instance beet salad or *palcan salatasi* and sweet cream with vegetables or *asure* from Turkey, mint cheese or *laban* and flaky pastry with pistachios or balurieh from Syria, sweet rich cream of rice or *mighli* from Lebanon, chicken with orange and honey or *takiya auff* from Israel. From Egypt there is cabbage with vinegar or *kromb mikhallet* and vermicelli with raisins and fruit or *chariya*, from Libya mallow salad or *bekula*, from Tunisia scented semolina cake or *farka*, from Algeria snails with orange or *babouche* and from Morocco cumin soup or *harira bel karouya*.

Their common features sometimes give the tourist the impression that all oriental and North African cooking tastes alike, while that of the north may seem more varied. In fact, this is not so, although indeed nuances are greater in the west and flavors are less often blended.

A Santorin vineyard.
The vine-plants lying against the ground absorb the volcanic soil's sulfur that gives this wine its particular taste.
Grape-picking in the vineyards of the southern Bekaa plain, in Lebanese Druze country.
Grapes from the Roussillon region of France. A small part of the harvest, usually the second choice,
is set aside to be sun dried as raisins, as are Ionian Island currants.

◁ Some "eastern" dishes
found in Greece, Lebanon
and the Maghrib, such as tabouli,
sheep cheese, stuffed eggplants,
pureed chick peas and steamed semolina.

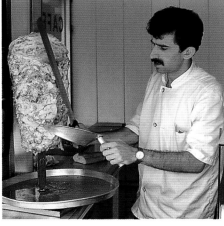

Street venders propose
to passers-by Greek gyros or Turkish
döner kebab, thin slices from a piece of
meat roasting on a vertical skewer
in front of cinders or, in the more
modern version, electric elements.

7

R.Campana

MASTERPIECES OF THE MEDITERRANEAN

The Mediterranean area has witnessed the birth, growth and death of more civilizations than any other region in the world. It can be considered a melting pot for modern cultures, which have, in one way or another, drawn their inspiration from the same prestigious historical past. Some of mankind's most beautiful artistic achievements can be found within this area, the fruit of a permanent fusion of ideas and art from the east and west. It is fitting that the last chapter of this book on the Mediterranean and the exceptional wealth of its cultures be devoted to the accomplishments the genius of its peoples have brought forth.

The six colossal monolithic shafts of the original fifty-four columns
in the Great Temple of Jupiter Helipolitan in Baalbek are all over twenty meters high.

Main entrance of the Temple of Bacchus also known as the Temple of Mysteries. ▷

THE EXTRAVAGANT TEMPLES AT BAALBEK AND DIDYMA

Greek and Roman vestiges are plentiful in the Mediterranean basin. Each culture left such a strong imprint during its respective era that the two alone seem to embody all of ancient history. Places once inhabited by Greeks and Romans abound with their palaces, temples, towns, private homes, street and ports. Outside Italy and Greece, particularly in the Middle East, artists showed great skill in combining the poetic refinement of the Greeks with the rational grandeur of the Romans, giving birth to original art forms that incarnate the best of both worlds. The temples in Asia Minor and Baalbek in Lebanon, the two largest architectural complexes dedicated to Olympian gods, are both striking illustrations.

THE TEMPLES AT BAALBEK

The ruins of Baalbek are located in the Bekaa plain at the foot of the Anti-Lebanon Range, 85 kilometers east of Beirut. They are reminders of the most grandiose sanctuaries the Romans ever built. The town of Baalbek itself dates back to the remotest times. According to an ancient Semitic legend it is the oldest town on earth, built by Cain himself as protection against God's wrath. Another has it that these cyclopean monuments had to have been erected by giants sent by King Nimrod. This belief is due to the presence in the surrounding wall of the famous Trilithon or 'temple of the three stones', a unit formed by three enormous stones resting on blocks that are most imposing, forming a colonnade 6 meters above the ground. These blocks were extracted from nearby quarries and each is 19 or 20 meters long and 4 meters in width and height. Their average weight is 830 tons! Many historians believe they date back to the time of the Giblites in Phoenicia, but this hypothesis is not unanimously accepted. Whatever the origin, the fact remains that monumental proportions are a time honored tradition in Baalbek.

The Baalbek site is known to have had several sanctuaries during early ancient times, but no pre-Roman monument has survived. Nor does anything remain of the 250-year Seleucid occupation of the city they called Heliopolis. Baalbek means 'Lord of the Bekaa,' a god of the earth often incorrectly assimilated with the Syrian-Phoenician sun god, Baal. It was during the Roman occupation that the city reached its pinnacle. In 66 BC the Consul Pompey seized Syria and Palestine and shortly thereafter, Caesar established a colony in Baalbek that he baptized Julia after his daughter. In the following years, Roman settlers began to build the largest temples of the era, in order to impress the local population with the omnipotence of Rome. It took two centuries to complete the construction. Several emperors, particularly Septimius Severus and Caracalla, contributed magnanimously to the undertaking, intending that it be a showcase for Roman wealth and power. The two main temples, one dedicated to Jupiter-Hadad, a fusion of the Roman and Syrian sun gods and the other to Atargatis or to Bacchus, were completed in the first and second centuries respectively. Smaller sanctuaries, such as the temple of Mercury or the round temple of Venus were built at the same time. Emperor Hadrian protected the city with high walls some of which still remain.

Christianity came to Baalbek as early as the second century and triumphed one hundred years later, during the reign of Justinian. The emperor had a basilica built at the entrance to the temple of Jupiter and forbade worship in the other

*General view of the large Temple of Jupiter with its "tower-altars;"
in the background, the walls of the hexagonal forecourt.*

*The Temple of Bacchus is built on a five-meter-high podium.
The peripteral shape of the Temples of Bacchus and Jupiter are unusual for Roman sanctuaries.*

temples. Within a short time, the whole Baalbek temple complex fell into disuse. Later the Arabs, followed by the Ottomans, constructed fortifications around it. Over the course of the centuries, the inhabitants of the region plundered the temples, stealing stones to build their own houses. The death knell for the Baalbek sanctuaries was sounded in 1318 and 1759 when two terrible earthquakes devastated the region. The awesome majesty of the Baalbek temples is partially due to their monumental proportions, but also to the fusion of Greco-Roman and Syrian-Asian styles. In front of the temple of Jupiter, which was constructed on a 14-meter-high podium, is a large 51-step propylaea, or entranceway, leading to a hexagonal forecourt 62 meters in diameter, followed by a immense raised rectangular court measuring 2,110 square meters. Six columns with three drums of the original 54 in the south peristyle remain. Their shafts are 2.20 meters in diameter and twenty meters high, the highest in the world. By comparison, those of the Parthenon in Athens are only 7.30 meters high.

Fifty meters south of the temple of Jupiter-Hadad rises the temple of Mercury or of Atargatis, Hadad's consort. Specialists still debate to which deity the sanctuary was dedicated. It is often referred to as the 'small temple' compared to its giant neighbor. Yet, its dimensions are impressive. It is surrounded by a three-meter-wide gallery supported by a colonnade that originally consisted of 50 columns, each over 18 meters high. An elaborate entablature surmounted by a sumptuous cornice runs above the monumental capitals. Curved slabs comprise the superb sculpted coffered ceiling of the gallery. The entrance portico is 6.5 meters wide and 15 meters high and its jambs are covered with Corinthian ornaments, rope molding and cereal, fruit and grape patterns. The lintel, decorated with an eagle holding Mercury's wand in its claws, is the most beautiful the ancients have bequeathed to us.

Ancient texts were unanimous in praising the splendor of the Baalbek sanctuary ceilings.
The Temple of Bacchus, which is decorated with a surprising series of Jewish stars and busts of gods,
satyrs and maenads, is considered a representative example.

Although this dipteral Hellenistic temple at Didyma was never completed, the visitor can but be impressed by the alignment
of 120 sculpted pedestals of the exterior columns, each of which is nearly 20 meters high.

Of the many monumental effigies
that enhanced the temple friezes only two Gorgons remain intact

DIDYMA

Around ten miles south of Miletus on the Aegean coast of Turkey, not far from the modern village of Yenihisar, appear the ruins of the Didymaeum, the imposing sanctuary dedicated to Apollo Philesios. Although practically in ruins, the size of the monument creates a feeling of admiration and

alone. At first allied cities agreed to help, but they were unable to maintain their financial contributions. For over four hundred years, thousands of slaves and workers sporadically came from Greece, Asia Minor and the Orient to work, whenever funds were available. There were further difficulties

astonishment in the visitor. One thousand years before the Christian era, the place was known for its oracles. Held to be sacred, it sheltered several small sanctuaries dedicated to the gods of the earth and sky. By the seventh century BC, the Branchids, a caste of priests believed to be descendants of Branchus, the mythical founder of the religious center, had bestowed on the site a reputation that spread far beyond the boundaries of Asia Minor. The Didymaeum was first erected in honor of the god Apollo. It quickly became as famous as the sanctuary at Delphi, attracting pilgrims from all over the Greek world. Around 540 BC the powerful city of Miletus annexed, developed and embellished it and its reputation spread further throughout the Mediterranean basin. It was plundered and burnt to the ground during the Persian invasion of 494 BC, when much to the inhabitants' fury, the Branchid priests delivered a statue of the god by Kanachos of Sicyône into the hands of the enemy. This was the demise of the first version of the Didymaeum. The revival of the Didymaeum was the work of Alexander the Great, who drove out the Persians in 334 AD. The inhabitants of Miletus decided to build a new, larger more beautiful temple. This undertaking, initiated by Paeonios of Epheus and Daphnis of Miletus, proved to be extravagant, since the colossal size of the second temple and the inordinate sums of money its construction required were in fact challenges too great for the province of Miletus to bear

when the Galatians attacked during the third century BC, followed by pirate incursions that lasted for two hundred years. Fortunately, the Romans, under the impetus of the emperors Caesar, Caligula, Trajan and Hadrian, decided to continue construction, adding the well-known Hellenistic rigor. The Didymaeum was almost finished when the Goths plundered it in 256 AD. The Milesians and Romans courageously set to work again and soon built a third sanctuary upon the ruins. Unfortunately, in 392 the Roman Emperor converted to Christianity and the work in Didyma and other sites was abandoned. Emperor Justinian, however, struck by the majestic beauty of the temple, decided to finish partially what had been undertaken, before transforming it into a fortress! Finally, an earthquake destroyed what was left of the temple in the tenth and eleventh centuries. The ruins of the temple to Apollo that remain are impressive. Three of the original 120 twenty-meter-high columns are still standing and the mixture of styles has produced some surprising effects. The conception of the podium and the Ionic bases of the façade are unusual when compared to classical standards for Greek temples. At first glance the storied angle capitals, the splendid Gorgon-head friezes, the palm leaf dentils, the 'caissons' with effigies of the gods seem out of place in a Hellenistic context. They reflect, of course, the oriental influence and contribute to the phenomenally elegant grandeur of the entire site.

Many details, such as the Greek borders decorating the pedestals or the bulls' heads on the capitals, show the blending of oriental and western traditions.

The facade of the Palace of the Grand Masters,
destroyed during a gunpowder factory explosion in 1856, was entirely rebuilt by the Italians before World War II.

The facade of the imposing Knights Hospital,
is the original one, built during the second half of the fifteenth century. ▷

STRENGTH
THE CITADEL OF RHODES
AND KRAK DES CHEVALIERS

The era of the Crusades, with the massive incursion of European Christians in the Muslim-dominated Near East, provided architects of both camps with opportunities to build fortresses and castles to demonstrate to the enemy their master's strength. Among the western powers, France and Italy showed the greatest ingenuity. A series of castles and fortified places constituted a line of defense stretching from the western Aegean Islands to Cyprus and topped the hillcrests of Syria and Palestine. For three hundred years, from the eleventh to the thirteenth centuries, these fortresses symbolized western omnipotence. Krak des Chevaliers and the citadel of the Grand Masters in Rhodes are two of the most impressive examples.

THE CITADEL OF RHODES

Located in the southeastern Aegean, Rhodes is the largest of the Dodecanese Islands. According to the legend, it was given, in the shape of the nymph Rhodia, to the god of the sun, Apollo Phoebus. In the seventh century BC a brilliant civilization flourished there, rapidly colonizing the neighboring islands. Three centuries later, despite competition and occasional attacks from the Macedonians and then the Romans, Rhodes became the main maritime and trading power of the eastern Mediterranean. Its noted schools of art created masterpieces including the renowned Colossos completed in 265 by Chares of Lindos. After this era of grandeur, Rhodes practically fell into oblivion as aggressive merchant fleets from the west secured economic dominance over those of the east. Rhodes regained its strategic and spiritual importance in 1306 with the arrival of Foulques de Villaret and the Knights of Saint John of Jerusalem (Knights Hospitalers), whom the Muslims had forced out of Palestine. This order had been founded in the eleventh century to receive and protect pilgrims in the holy places. They had built a hospital in Jerusalem and had erected a powerful fortress in Saint-Jean d'Acre. When the Turks captured the latter in 1291, the Knights were obliged to leave the Holy Land. They took refuge first on Cyprus, and then Rhodes, which was a Genovese possession at the time. Here they constructed an advanced Christian bastion against the Muslim threat to the east. In only a few decades the Knights built new ports, cities and fortified walls. In Rhodes City they constructed an enormous town whose northern third, fortified on all four sides, came to be called collachium or the citadel, where the Knights lived under the authority of successive grand masters. Despite the upheavals that have affected the island since then, the citadel surprises the visitor by the size of its monuments and the feeling of power generated by the high walls. There are four monumental gates of entry, each bearing the shield of arms of the person who commissioned it. Knights Road leads to the Palace of the Grand Masters along a cobblestone street lined with 'inns,' Gothic buildings bearing coats of arms where the Knights lived by language group. The order was divided into seven 'languages' or nations: Aragon, England, Auvergne, Castille, France, Italy and Provence, each governed by a bailiff. The French were the most numerous and a Grand Master from among their ranks directed the entire citadel. Standing at the end of the street is the majestic Palace of the Grand Masters, which used to be a fortress with moats, battlements,

a keep and three stories of underground storerooms for arms and munitions. The other important building in the citadel is the Knights' Hospital, which now serves as a museum. Its construction was begun in 1440 and completed under Pierre d'Aubusson, the Grand Master from 1478 to 1505. The main ward was divided into two naves and could accommodate one hundred patients at the same time. They were assigned to thirty-two collective beds, an absolute record for the time! Despite the fact that Rhodes changed hands four times - the Turkish occupation by Süleyman the Magnificent in 1522, the Italian occupation in 1911, the Germans between 1943 and 1945, and finally the English until 1948 - the collachium as a whole has suffered little damage and appears almost as it was at its heyday.

View of the ramparts west of the collachium and the Palace of the Grand Masters.
The medieval walls that circle the old city for four kilometers were constructed in the fourteenth century
then reinforced several times, notably by Pierre d'Aubusson.

The former arsenal has become the Museum of Decorative Arts.

The famous Knights Street is a long straight thoroughfare leading to the Palace of the Grand Masters.
It is lined with the handsomest civilian buildings in the collachium,
namely the inns of the different nations represented in the Order of the Knights.

This massive fortress, the Krak des Chevaliers, known as Qal'at al-Hisn by the Arabs,
dominates the coastal plain of Al Buqaua.
It was built from an old fort, the donjon des Akrades, which fell into Crusader hands in 1099.

Krak des Chevaliers

Known as Qal'at al-Hisn by the Arabs, Krak des Chevaliers (krak is Kurdish for castle), the exceptional Syrian fortress, is the best preserved fortress in the Middle East. At an altitude of 750 meters, it dominates the Kabir Valley and the Al Bukaïa plain. It was built by the Crusaders on the site of a old Kurdish fort called the keep of the Akrades, which had been constructed fortress. Finally in 1271, the European garrison, starving after a long siege, was forced to surrender to the Mamluk sultan Baybars, who added towers to the original fortifications, creating a mixture of European and Arab styles.

The fortress is divided into three parts, the outer ramparts, the inside wall and the central building. There were thirteen

on the ruins of a citadel dating from several centuries before the beginning of the Christian era. The strategic location of the site was certainly exceptional, overlooking the only pass in the mountain chain stretching along the Mediterranean coast from Antakya in Turkey to Beirut in Lebanon. Whoever controlled this breach was master of the military and trade routes of the region.

In 1099, the crusaders under Raymond de Saint-Gilles, Count of Toulouse, seized the keep of the Akrades. Tancred's followers succeeded them, followed by the Knights of St. John (Hospitalers) in 1142. The history of the fortress included several violent earthquakes and frequent Muslim attacks. The crusaders reconstructed, enlarged and equipped it with sturdy defensive works. They dug wells within the perimeter of the walls, making it possible for the soldiers to endure long sieges. By the beginning of the thirteenth century, it had become the largest stronghold of the Christian world. A garrison of three to four thousand men could be sheltered within its fortifications. For over half a century its defenders resisted continuous sieges and assaults without damage to the powerful

towers spaced at regular intervals above the high walls. The main entrance located on the east, leads to a gently sloping ramp by which mounted knights entered. After the guardroom and the stables, the ramp makes a right angle turn and opens onto the second wall, separated from the ramparts by deep moats whose water was originally used for filling baths and refreshing horses. The most remarkable of the several large towers protecting the second wall is the Princess's Tower, with its three rows of trefled arches and a large cantilevered gallery from which stones and burning oil could be poured onto the assailants.

Inside the last wall lies the castle's open courtyard. The experience of walking along the seven ogival bays of the west gallery, lingering in the long vaulted rooms (the largest is 120 meters) and visiting the kitchens, the refectory, the church, the storerooms and the upstairs rooms is an unmitigated pleasure.

Having resisted centuries of assaults practically undamaged, Krak des Chevaliers is one of the principal attractions for tourists visiting Syria.

Three details of the architecture of the fortified castle: the powerful wall of the central building surrounded by moats, the ogival bays of the gallery and the long vaulted entrance ramp.

General view of Kykko monastery hidden within the Troodos oak and pine forests.

Cypriot monks continue the century-old art of icon making, using pure gold for illumination. ▷

REFINEMENT
THE KYKKO MONASTERY
AND THE ALHAMBRA PALACE

The Mediterranean region abounds with religious monuments. More than one-third of the world's sanctuaries, of all faiths, is located here. Between the fifth and the fifteenth centuries the two greatest revealed religions, Christianity and Islam, constructed more churches, basilicas, and mosques in the Mediterranean basin than all the temples and sanctuaries other religions had erected over the course of 4,000 years. Eastern and western influences were constantly intermixing, resulting in buildings whose refinement is equaled only by their wealth. Foremost among them are the Alhambra in Grenada, Spain, built by the Moors, and the monastery of Kykko, constructed by Orthodox Christians in Cyprus.

THE KYKKO MONASTERY

In the heart of Cyprus, thirteen kilometers from the village of Pedulas, suspended on the mountainside, rises the imposing monastery of Kykko, the richest and the most renowned of the island. Some say its name originated with the Greek word *kokkonyes* or oak tree, thousands of which cover the neighboring mountains. It was founded in 1100 by Byzantine monks during the reign of Emperor Alexius Comnenus and is dedicated to the Virgin Mary. Tradition has it that the head monk, whose name was Isaïas, chose the spot following a divine revelation, constructing the first buildings with money he had received from the emperor for healing his daughter's sciatica. Isaïas is also believed to have installed here the famous icon of the Virgin and Child, one of the three holy images attributed to Saint Luke. The gilded icon is locked in a tortoise-shell mother-of-pearl casket that is kept in the iconostasis, lit by ostrich-egg lamps hanging from the ceiling, as is the custom in Cypriot sanctuaries. It is the most venerated icon of Cyprus and one of the most famous of the Eastern Orthodox world. An aura of mystery surrounds it, for it is believed to possess great power, such as rainmaking, which brings crowds of farmers to Kykko to implore intervention during the long periods of drought. Near the iconostasis is an array of miraculous relics.

One bronze arm is believed to have belonged to a man who tried to light his pipe at the lamp that burns continuously before the icon. A swordfish-shaped ornament is said to be the offering of a Greek sailor the Virgin Mary saved from drowning. The holy image is shown to the public on August 15th and September 8th, the important religious holidays that attract millions of pilgrims from Cyprus, and as far away as Greece and Russia. Large fairs are held at this time.

The original monastery was partially destroyed several times by earthquakes and Turkish pillaging. In 1813 a great fire laid waste to the chapels and most of the prayer rooms and monastic cells, destroying irreplaceable masterpieces. Each time catastrophe struck, however, the monks patiently rebuilt the monastery with the aid of the faithful. Most of the main buildings one admires today date back to the nineteenth century. They are painted white, and have been carefully restored, offering the visitor the incomparable sight of minute paintings and refined mosaics in which sacred and profane have been intermixed to produce a baroque profusion of vivid colors and gold. The heavily laden, almost gaudy, decoration reflects Russian and Byzantine taste mixed with some typical Oriental details, in the animal and vegetal miniatures. Along the walls are two rows of Biblical scenes: episodes from Genesis and the main events

in the life of Christ. In contrast, the interiors of the monastic cells are simple and austere.

The Kykko monastery was the headquarters of a veritable financial and economic organization possessing real estate in Turkey and far off Russia. Although the order has lost all its foreign domains, it remains one of the major Cypriot landowners. The abbeys directing the monastery have always managed to guard their freedom and remain independent of the island's successive political powers. Over the course of the centuries, the monastery has earned itself a solid reputation for independence, and is even known as the only center of dissension in the eastern Mediterranean. The first president of the Republic of Cyprus, Archbishop Makarios III, was a novice here and insisted that his final resting place be near the sanctuary.

The first-floor gallery dominates the interior court of the church housing the holiest image of the Orthodox Church, an icon of the Virgin traditionally attribued to saint Luke.

The main entrance to the monastery.

Several sanctuaries, each of whose porch is decorated with superb paintings and sculptures, open onto the main court.

After being devastated by a terrible fire in 1813, the monastery was reconstructed and the paintings and mosaics were patiently restored. Thus, most of today's buildings are slightly over a century old, which explains their "new" look.

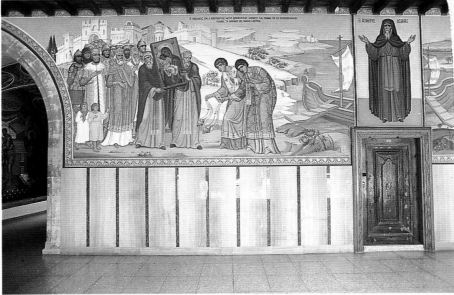

The heavy Baroque treatment of the mosaics and paintings clearly reveal a mixture of Byzantine, Russian and Greek tastes and contrast sharply with the austere monastic cells.

The majestic Sierra Nevada's snow-capped ridges dominate Grenada
and the Arab-Christian architectural wonder, the Alhambra that overlooks the city.
The graceful Nasrid constructions blend harmoniously
with the imposing Renaissance-style palace of Charles V.

The Alhambra in Grenada

In the twelfth century, after dethroning the Almoravid dynasty, the Almohads of Ibn Tumart, a Berber from North Africa, invaded southern Spain, where the Muslims had established their dominion four centuries earlier. A brilliant new civilization was born during the reigns of these new masters. Early in the eighth century, Mohammed I, a Nasrid serving the Almohads, had taken the title of Commander of the Believers and decided to found his own kingdom in the area of Grenada. He became the first of a new Nasrid dynasty, which would reign over the tiny kingdom of Grenada, Almeria, Cadix and Malaga for three centuries. He had many prestigious monuments erected in the capital, and had the first edifice of the future Alhambra built on a hilltop overlooking the city. The site had originally contained small Iberian and Roman forts upon whose ruins the conquering Arabs had built a fortified place in 711, when they captured the city. It was, however, Mohammed I's descendants, Yusuf I and in particular his son,

Mohammed V, who were responsible for the architectural marvel called the Alhambra or 'the red,' derived from the color of its stonework. The kingdom of Grenada was the last Muslim stronghold in Spain. Despite desperate resistance, it fell to the coalition of Christian kings led by Charles V in 1492.

The Alhambra dominates the city of Grenada and gives it its character. It was altered several times, and also enlarged, and embellished by successive rulers. It consists of the Alcazaba fortress, the oldest part of the Alhambra, and the Alcazar palace. The thirteenth century Alcazaba citadel has massive outer walls that originally included twenty-four towers linked by a curtain wall. The Alcazar palace was constructed in the fourteenth century. Despite the fragility of the building materials sculpted stucco on the outside and marble paneling lining the interior it has resisted the elements. It was designed according to a North African model, around three interior courts, each with a precise function: the Mexuar court leading to the diwan where the sultan handed down justice, the Court of the Myrtles in the center of the palace with its rectangular basin surrounded by myrtles and opening directly onto the Hall of the Ambassadors, and finally the Court of the Lions adjacent to the harem. The Court of the Myrtles is the perfect

Generalife and the Machuca Palace. The former, organized around the large Court of the Acequaia, was the Nasrid rulers' summer residence. It contains superb spacious gardens with large basins and fountains. The Machuca Palace is a charming Italianate palace built for King Charles V by the architect Pedro Machuca.

example of classical Muslim architecture. The large basin in the middle is framed at each end by porticos of seven semi-circular arches that carry the regular delicately carved arcades of the upper story. The Court of the Lions is a masterpiece in its own right. Its name comes from the famous fountain in its center; twelve marble lions spitting out water support a large basin. The rectangular court has been laid with flowerbeds and is surrounded by a gallery with delicately sculpted pillars and arcades. The walls are tiled and adorned with finely carved stucco. The four side doors give access to magnificently decorated rooms and vestibules. The examples of plaster sculpture, ceramic panels, gold-leaf Koranic inscriptions, carved cedar ceilings and stalactite stucco and marble cupolas are endless. Visitors favor the Barca Hall, with its magnificent carved wooden ceiling, the star-studded octagonal Abencerrage cupola, the Kings' Hall, with its stalactite hemispheral arches and cupolas and the delicately sculpted stucco decoration in the Hall of the Two Sisters. Two other outlying buildings are also worth mentioning: the

The Alhambra's originality lies in the liberty the fourteenth century architects took with the Arab rules of construction, undoubtedly acting under orders of the Nasrid sovereigns. They were, thus, unrestrained by the ethereal rigor and unique style the Prophet's descendants had imposed, and could indulge in the innovations and refinement popular in the contemporary Muslim world. To the traditional architectural elements of arabesques, geometrical and spiral patterns inherited from the Abbassid, Fatimid and Seljuk schools, they added palmettes, rosettes, chrysoles, lanceoles, cornucopias, plants and flowers, in the new styles of the Mamluk, Persian and Mongol artists. The many epigraphic patterns that decorate the walls follow the same inspiration. Alongside the rigid traditional inscriptions in Kufic that were fashionable during the Ommiad dynasty, appeared the new, more sinuous decorative cursive writings, Neskhi and Maghribi.

The Alhambra has given its name to the Moorish decorative and architectural style considered the epitome of the Muslim spirit in Europe.

◁ One of the entrances to the Alcazaba fortress, the oldest portion of the Alhambra,
built by Muhammad ibn Yusuf ibn Nasr in the twelfth century.

◁ The Comares Court, also known as the Court of the Myrtles,
is surrounded with arcaded galleries whose reflections can be seen in the large rectangular pool.

The masterpiece of Moorish art in Spain,
the fourteenth-century Court of the Lions, named for the twelve marble lions that support the central basin.
The delicately sculptured galleries that frame the court open onto four superbly decorated rooms.

CONCLUSION

THE MEDITERRANEAN IS NOT UNIQUE, BUT INFINITE. THERE IS NOT ONE SINGLE MEDITERRANEAN LANDSCAPE, BUT MULTIPLE MEDITERRANEAN LANDSCAPES; NOT A SINGLE MAN OR WOMAN'S FACE THAT ALONE RESUMES THE MEDITERRANEAN TYPE, BUT SEVERAL. THERE IS NOT ONE SINGLE CIVILIZATION, BUT A SUCCESSION OF MANY CIVILIZATIONS WHICH HAVE FOUGHT, ALLIED AND MERGED. THE MEDITERRANEAN IS NOT EVEN A SINGLE SEA, BUT RATHER THE JUXTAPOSITION OF SEVERAL SMALL SEAS. THE MEDITERRANEAN BASIN IS RICH PRECISELY BECAUSE OF THESE MULTIPLE DIFFERENCES AND CONTRASTS, ALL NUANCES OF THE SAME SPIRIT. INDEED, THE MIRACLE OF THE REGION IS TO HAVE PRODUCED A SINGLE SPIRIT, COMMON TO ALL THE PEOPLE OF THE MEDITERRANEAN SINCE THE DAWN OF HUMANITY, DESPITE THE WARS AND RELIGIOUS AND ECONOMIC RIVALRIES THAT HAVE DIVIDED THEM. WHEN A MEDITERRANEAN PERSON IS FAR FROM HIS NATIVE LAND, HE FEELS AT HOME EVERYWHERE IN THE REGION FROM GIBRALTAR TO ALEXANDRIA, FROM CUETA TO ATHENS OR FROM VENICE TO BEIRUT. PHOENICIAN RUINS BECKON TO US IN LEBANON, AS THEY DO IN CARTHAGE. ONE IS CERTAIN TO FIND VESTIGES OF GREEK AND ROMAN CIVILIZATION IN TURKEY AND SYRIA, JUST AS THE ARAB TOUCH INEVITABLY CAN BE FELT IN SPAIN, SICILY AND MALTA. THE VENETIAN PRESENCE IS EVIDENT FROM SICILY TO RHODES AND IN CONTINENTAL AND INSULAR GREECE. MEN ARE NO EXCEPTION TO THE RULE. THE NORTH AFRICAN PHYSICAL TYPE APPEARS IN THE FEATURES OF SOUTHERN SPANIARDS, SICILIANS, CALABRIANS AND CRETANS, WHILE THE SKIN COLOR AND THE LIGHT EYES OF SOME LEBANESE, TURKS AND EGYPTIANS ATTEST TO THE PAST PRESENCE IN THEIR COUNTRIES OF WESTERN PEOPLES. THE SAME IS TRUE OF ALL THE RELIGIONS THAT, DESPITE SINISTER RIVALRIES, ACCEPT THEIR MUTUAL PRESENCE IN CITIES AROUND THE MEDITERRANEAN. THERE ARE JEWISH QUARTERS IN GRENADA, GENOA, TUNIS AND VALLETTA, AND TUNISIAN, ALGERIAN AND MOROCCAN QUARTERS IN THE CENTERS OF THE LARGE CHRISTIAN CITIES SUCH AS MAZARA DEL VALLO, BARCELONA, MARSEILLE, NAPLES AND ATHENS. LARGE POPULATIONS OF CHRISTIANS LIVE IN DAMASCUS, CAIRO AND JERUSALEM WHILE ORTHODOX CHRISTIANS AND ROMAN CATHOLICS ARE PRESENT IN GREECE, CYPRUS AND ISTANBUL. PALESTINIANS LIVE IN ISRAEL AND VICE VERSA.

ALL OF THIS GOES TO MAKE UP THE MEDITERRANEAN SPIRIT: A SHARED CLIMATE, ABUNDANT SUNSHINE AND A CLOSENESS TO NATURE THAT CORRESPOND TO THE PHYSICAL, PSYCHOLOGICAL AND MORAL TRAITS OF THE MEN AND WOMEN OF THE REGION. THIS HAS PRODUCED THE SHARED CERTAINTY OF BELONGING TO THE SAME UNIQUE WORLD, IN SPITE OF DIFFERENCES AMONG NEIGHBORS. IT IS AS DIFFICULT TO PRESERVE THEIR WAY OF LIFE, HOWEVER, AS IT IS TO PROTECT THE EARTH'S LIVING SPECIES AND TO RESIST THE MODERN WORLD. IN A WORLD ECONOMY WITH THE SOPHISTICATED MEANS OF COMMUNICATIONS

"The youth of the world can always be found along the same shores...
Those of us who live around the Mediterranean share the same light.   In the heart of the European night,
the sunny/sunlight thoughts/ideas, the dual civilization awaits its dawn."
(Albert Camus, "The Rebel," Thought at the Meridian).

THAT HAVE REDUCED THE GLOBE TO ONE HUGE SUBURB, WHAT CHANCÉS DOES THE MEDITERRANEAN AREA, THE ATTRACTIVE MARE NOSTRUM OF THE ROMANS, HAVE OF KEEPING ITS AUTHENTICITY? IS THERE STILL ANY REASONABLE HOPE THAT THE GODS, WHETHER BAAL OR JUPITER, OR MOLOCH OR AMON, ARE LIKELY TO EXERT THEIR INFLUENCE ALONGSIDE OF YAHWEH=GOD=ALLAH TO SAVE THEIR SINGULAR PLACE OF BIRTH.

Conception Graphic realisation
© BOWER
3 place aux huiles - 13001 Marseille

Photocomposition, execution and cartography
© PLEIN FORMAT
72 boulevard Notre Dame - 13006 Marseille

Photogravure
CITIEMME
corso Svizzera, 185 - Turin

Impression
EGEDSA
Rois de Corella,12, 16, Nave 1
08205 Sabadell /Barcelone)

© 1997 VILO -
25 rue Ginoux - 75015 Paris

Printed in Egedsa
in september, 1997
Dépôt légal, september, 1997

ISBN 271 91 0345-4